The Biggest Wars in History

Crafted by Skriuwer

Copyright © 2024 by Skriuwer.

All rights reserved. No part of this book may be used or reproduced in any form whatsoever without written permission except in the case of brief quotations in critical articles or reviews.

For more information, contact : **kontakt@skriuwer.com** (www.skriuwer.com)

Table of Contents

Chapter 1: Introduction to Global Conflicts

- 1.1 The Definition of War
- 1.2 The Causes of War
- 1.3 The Impact of War on Society
- 1.4 Measuring the Scale of War
- 1.5 Overview of the World's Biggest Wars

Chapter 2: The Peloponnesian War

- 2.1 Origins of the Conflict
- 2.2 Key Battles and Strategies
- 2.3 The Role of Leadership
- 2.4 The War's Aftermath
- 2.5 The Legacy of the Peloponnesian War

Chapter 3: The Punic Wars

- 3.1 Rome vs. Carthage: The Struggle for the Mediterranean
- 3.2 The First Punic War
- 3.3 The Second Punic War
- 3.4 The Third Punic War and the Destruction of Carthage
- 3.5 The Impact of the Punic Wars

Chapter 4: The Mongol Conquests

- 4.1 Genghis Khan and the Rise of the Mongol Empire
- 4.2 The Conquest of China
- 4.3 The Invasion of the Islamic World
- 4.4 The European Campaigns
- 4.5 The Legacy of the Mongol Empire

Chapter 5: The Hundred Years' War

- 5.1 The Origins of the Conflict
- 5.2 The Early Phase: Edwardian War
- 5.3 The Role of Joan of Arc
- 5.4 The Lancastrian Phase and the End of the War
- 5.5 The Impact on France and England

Chapter 6: The Thirty Years' War

- 6.1 The Religious and Political Causes
- 6.2 Major Campaigns and Battles
- 6.3 The Role of Foreign Powers
- 6.4 The Peace of Westphalia
- 6.5 The Long-Term Consequences

Chapter 7: The Napoleonic Wars

- 7.1 The Rise of Napoleon Bonaparte
- 7.2 The War of the Third Coalition
- 7.3 The Peninsular War and the Invasion of Russia
- 7.4 The Fall of Napoleon
- 7.5 The Legacy of the Napoleonic Wars

Chapter 8: The American Civil War

- 8.1 The Causes of the Civil War
- 8.2 Major Battles and Campaigns
- 8.3 The Role of Abraham Lincoln
- 8.4 The Emancipation Proclamation
- 8.5 The Reconstruction Era

Chapter 9: World War I

- 9.1 The Origins of the Great War
- 9.2 Trench Warfare and Major Battles
- 9.3 The Role of Technology in WWI
- 9.4 The Global Impact of the War
- 9.5 The Treaty of Versailles and Its Consequences

Chapter 10: World War II

- 10.1 The Rise of Fascism and the Road to War
- 10.2 Major Theaters of War
- 10.3 The Holocaust and War Crimes
- 10.4 The Role of Allied Leaders
- 10.5 The Aftermath of WWII

Chapter 11: The Korean War

- 11.1 The Origins of the Korean Conflict
- 11.2 Major Battles and Military Strategies
- 11.3 The Role of International Powers
- 11.4 The Armistice and Its Aftermath
- 11.5 The Legacy of the Korean War

Chapter 12: The Vietnam War

- 12.1 The Origins of the Vietnam Conflict
- 12.2 Major Military Campaigns
- 12.3 The Role of the Media
- 12.4 The Anti-War Movement
- 12.5 The Fall of Saigon and Its Consequences

Chapter 13: The Gulf War

- 13.1 The Lead-Up to War
- 13.2 Operation Desert Storm
- 13.3 The Role of Technology
- 13.4 The Aftermath of the War
- 13.5 The Gulf War's Place in Modern Military History

Chapter 14: The War on Terror

- 14.1 The Origins of the War on Terror
- 14.2 The Afghanistan Conflict
- 14.3 The Iraq War
- 14.4 Counterterrorism Strategies
- 14.5 The Ongoing Global Impact

Chapter 15: Conclusion and Reflections

- 15.1 The Evolution of Warfare
- 15.2 Lessons Learned from History's Biggest Wars
- 15.3 The Human Cost of War
- 15.4 The Future of Warfare
- 15.5 Final Thoughts on Peace and Conflict

Chapter 1

Introduction to Global Conflicts

The Definition of War

War is a complex and multifaceted phenomenon that has shaped human history throughout the ages. At its core, war can be defined as a conflict between organized groups, typically characterized by the use of armed force. This definition, however, is but a starting point. The classification of war involves various dimensions, including the nature of the conflict, the parties involved, the scale of violence, and the objectives pursued.

To understand what constitutes a war, it is essential to explore its fundamental characteristics. Generally, war can be delineated from other forms of conflict by its organized nature, which involves formal or informal combatants engaging in sustained violence. The entities involved may include nation-states, insurgent groups, or coalitions of different factions, each with defined political or territorial goals. The intensity of violence is also a critical factor; wars are typically marked by significant casualties and destruction, distinguishing them from lesser forms of conflict such as skirmishes or police actions.

Wars can be classified in several ways, one of the most common being the distinction between interstate and intrastate wars. Interstate wars occur between two or more sovereign states, often over issues like territory, resources, or ideological differences. Examples include the World Wars, where multiple nations engaged in expansive conflicts with global implications. On the other hand, intrastate wars, often termed civil wars, occur within a single state, typically involving government forces and non-state actors vying for power or autonomy. The American Civil War and the Syrian Civil War are prominent examples of intrastate conflicts that have had lasting impacts on their respective societies.

Another important classification is based on the motivations behind the war. Wars can be categorized as aggressive or defensive. Aggressive wars are initiated by one party seeking to conquer or expand its territory, while defensive wars are fought to protect a nation from external threats. The moral and legal implications of these classifications can vary significantly, influencing international perceptions and responses to conflict.

Additionally, wars can be classified by their scale and duration. Major wars, such as World War I and World War II, are characterized by high levels of mobilization, extensive international involvement, and significant casualties, often resulting in profound geopolitical shifts. In contrast, limited wars may involve fewer resources and narrower objectives, such as conflicts over specific territories or issues. The distinction between total war, where all aspects of society are mobilized for the war effort, and limited war, where only specific sectors are engaged, is also essential in understanding the scope of a conflict.

The impact of technology on warfare has led to further classifications, such as conventional and unconventional warfare. Conventional warfare typically involves regular armies engaging in battle using traditional weapons and tactics, while unconventional warfare includes guerrilla tactics, cyber warfare, and terrorism, which have emerged as significant forms of conflict in the modern era.

Ultimately, the definition and classification of war are essential for comprehending its complexities and the consequences it bears on societies, economies, and cultures. Wars reshape borders, influence political ideologies, and often leave lasting scars on national identities. As we delve deeper into the study of war, it becomes clear that understanding its definitions and classifications not only provides insights into historical conflicts but also equips us to analyze ongoing and future wars in an increasingly interconnected world. The exploration of war's nature and classification is fundamental to understanding its role in shaping human history and the ongoing quest for peace.

The Causes of War

Wars have been a pervasive aspect of human civilization, shaping societies, economies, and cultures across the globe. Understanding the causes of war is vital to grasp how conflicts arise and develop over time. Historically, the causes of war can be categorized into several interrelated themes: political, economic, social, ideological, and territorial disputes.

Political Causes

One of the most prominent causes of war is political conflict. Wars often arise from struggles for power, control, and governance. This can manifest in various forms, including civil wars, where factions within a country vie for control, or international wars, where states engage in military conflict over political dominance. The Peloponnesian War, for instance, was primarily driven by the rivalry between Athens and Sparta, two powerful city-states in ancient Greece. Political ideologies also play a crucial role, as seen in the ideological battles of the 20th century, such as the clash between democratic nations and totalitarian regimes during World War II.

Economic Causes

Economic factors are frequently at the heart of warfare. Nations may engage in conflict to secure resources, control trade routes, or expand their markets. The Punic Wars exemplify this, as Rome and Carthage fought fiercely over control of the Mediterranean trade networks. Economic disparities, such as wealth inequality and competition for resources, can also incite conflict within and between nations. The quest for economic gain often drives nations to war, as they seek to protect or expand their economic interests at the expense of rivals.

Social Causes

Social tensions and grievances can lead to conflicts, especially when they involve issues of identity, ethnicity, or religion. Societies with deep-seated divisions are often more prone to violence. The Thirty Years' War, for example, was fueled by religious conflicts between Catholics and Protestants in Central Europe. Social causes are often interwoven with political and economic factors, as disenfranchised groups may resort to armed conflict to address systemic inequalities.

Ideological Causes

Ideological differences can also precipitate war, particularly when competing belief systems clash. The Cold War represents a contemporary example, where the capitalist West and the communist East engaged in a prolonged struggle for ideological supremacy, leading to various proxy wars around the globe. Ideologies can motivate societies to engage in conflict, with leaders often using ideological rhetoric to justify warfare and mobilize public support.

Territorial Causes

Territorial disputes are a common precursor to war, as nations seek to expand their borders or reclaim lost lands. The desire for territorial integrity can lead to conflicts, as seen in the Korean War, where the division of Korea along the 38th parallel resulted in a bitter and destructive war. Similarly, nationalist movements often arise from a desire for self-determination, leading to conflicts as groups seek to establish their own nation-states.

Conclusion

In summary, the causes of war are multifaceted and often interconnected. Political rivalries, economic competition, social grievances, ideological clashes, and territorial disputes can all serve as catalysts for conflict. Understanding these causes is essential for historians, policymakers, and societies at large, as it enables a deeper comprehension of the complexities surrounding warfare and the pursuit of peace. By analyzing the underlying reasons for past conflicts, we can glean lessons that may help prevent future wars and foster a more stable and harmonious world.

The Impact of War on Society

War is one of the most profound forces shaping human history, influencing societies, economies, and cultures in multifaceted ways. The consequences of war extend far beyond the battlefield, permeating through the very fabric of civilian life and often leaving lasting legacies that can alter the course of nations for generations. Understanding the impact of war on society entails examining several key dimensions: social structures, economic transformations, cultural shifts, and psychological effects.

Social Structures

Wars often catalyze significant changes in social hierarchies and structures. Historically, conflicts have acted as a leveling force, disrupting established social orders. For instance, during World War I and II, the mobilization of vast numbers of men and women into military service and wartime industries challenged traditional gender roles. Women took on roles that were previously deemed unsuitable or exclusive to men, leading to greater social acceptance of women in the workforce and laying the groundwork for future movements advocating for gender equality.

Moreover, wars frequently alter demographic compositions through displacement, migration, and loss of life. The aftermath of the Korean War, for example, resulted in the division of families and communities, leading to a lasting psychological and social impact that is still felt today. Post-war societies often grapple with the challenges of integrating returning soldiers, addressing the needs of war refugees, and dealing with the scars left on their social fabric.

Economic Transformations

Economically, wars can lead to both devastation and innovation. The immediate consequences of war often include destruction of infrastructure, industries, and agricultural systems, resulting in economic recession. However, the demand for military supplies can also stimulate production and technological advancements. For instance, World War II spurred significant innovations in technology, including advancements in aviation, medicine, and manufacturing processes, which contributed to post-war economic booms in several countries.

The concept of a "war economy" illustrates how nations can pivot their economic structures to support military efforts. Countries like the United States transitioned to wartime production, which not only created jobs but also expanded industrial capacities. The economic revitalization that followed conflicts can lead to substantial shifts in labor markets and economic policies.

Cultural Shifts
Culturally, wars have the power to reshape national identities and values. The narratives surrounding wars often lead to the creation of collective memories that bind communities together. For instance, the American Civil War fundamentally altered the national identity of the United States, fostering a sense of unity and purpose despite the divisions it initially revealed. The cultural artifacts, literature, art, and music that emerge from wartime experiences can reflect societal sentiments and influence future generations' perspectives on conflict and peace.

Moreover, wars can lead to a re-examination of moral and ethical values. The atrocities committed during conflicts, such as the Holocaust in World War II, have prompted global reflections on human rights, leading to the establishment of international laws and conventions aimed at preventing future atrocities.

Psychological Effects
The psychological impact of war on societies cannot be overstated. The trauma experienced by soldiers and civilians alike can lead to widespread mental health issues, such as PTSD, which affect not only individuals but also families and communities. The collective trauma can engender a culture of resilience but can also contribute to cycles of violence, as unresolved psychological issues manifest in various forms of social unrest.

In conclusion, the impact of war on society is profound and multifaceted, leading to significant transformations in social structures, economies, and cultures. While wars can yield immediate destruction and suffering, they can also catalyze change and progress. Understanding these dynamics is essential for grasping not only the history of human conflict but also the ongoing challenges societies face in the aftermath of war. Through careful reflection on the lessons of the past, societies can work toward fostering peace and mitigating the impacts of future conflicts.

Measuring the Scale of War
War has been an integral part of human history, shaping nations, economies, and social structures. However, not all conflicts carry the same weight or significance. To understand what makes a war "big," historians and analysts often measure it through three primary dimensions: casualties, duration, and global impact.

Casualties: The Human Cost
One of the most immediate and tangible ways to gauge the scale of a war is by examining the number of casualties it produces. This includes both military personnel and civilian deaths. Wars with high casualty rates often reflect intense and prolonged conflict, as seen in World War I and

World War II, which collectively resulted in tens of millions of deaths. For instance, World War II alone accounted for an estimated 70 to 85 million fatalities, making it one of the deadliest conflicts in human history.

Casualty figures provide insight not only into the scale of violence but also into the war's psychological and social ramifications. High casualty numbers can lead to trauma within societies, disrupt families, and create a legacy of grief that spans generations. Moreover, the impact of casualties is often felt beyond numbers; communities may be irrevocably changed as they grapple with loss and mourning.

Duration: The Test of Time

The length of a conflict is another critical factor in assessing its scale. Wars that span years or decades often reflect sustained social tensions and prolonged military engagements. The Hundred Years' War between England and France, which lasted from 1337 to 1453, serves as a prime example. Its extended duration not only drained resources but also deeply entrenched animosities and altered the political landscape of Europe.

Long wars tend to have compounding effects on societies, economies, and political structures. For example, the Thirty Years' War (1618-1648) devastated Central Europe, resulting in significant population loss and economic decline. The protracted nature of a conflict can lead to war fatigue among the populace, shifts in alliances, and changes in military strategies, all of which contribute to the war's legacy.

Global Impact: The Ripple Effect

While casualties and duration provide essential metrics, the global impact of a war is perhaps the most complex and far-reaching indicator of its scale. Wars that transcend national borders or involve multiple nations usually reshape international relations and geopolitical landscapes. World War II not only led to the emergence of the United States and the Soviet Union as superpowers but also established the United Nations as a platform for global governance and conflict resolution.

The global impact of a war can manifest in various forms, including economic ramifications, refugee crises, and shifts in cultural dynamics. For instance, the Vietnam War had profound implications not just for Vietnam but also for US foreign policy and domestic politics, igniting widespread anti-war movements and altering public perceptions of military intervention.

Additionally, some wars can lead to long-term changes in international norms and laws. The aftermath of World War II saw the establishment of the Geneva Conventions, which sought to regulate the conduct of armed conflict and protect civilian populations.

Conclusion

Measuring the scale of war requires a nuanced understanding of casualties, duration, and global impact. Each dimension contributes to a fuller picture of a conflict's significance and its lasting effects on society. As we reflect on history's biggest wars, it becomes clear that their consequences extend beyond the battlefield, influencing future generations in profound and often unforeseen ways. Understanding these factors allows us to analyze past conflicts critically and consider their implications for future warfare and international relations.

Overview of the World's Biggest Wars

The study of war is essential for understanding the complexities of human societies, their evolution, and the geopolitical landscape they inhabit. "The Biggest Wars in History" delves into some of the most significant conflicts that have shaped our world, each marked by unique causes, strategies, and consequences. This overview serves as a roadmap to the main wars explored in the book, highlighting their historical significance and the lessons they impart.

The Peloponnesian War (431-404 BCE) stands as a pivotal conflict in ancient history, representing the struggle between the democratic city-state of Athens and the militaristic Sparta. The war not only illustrates the dynamics of power and rivalry but also showcases the profound effects of leadership, epitomized by figures like Pericles and Lysander. Its aftermath reshaped the Greek world, leading to the decline of Athenian dominance and influencing later military and political thought.

The Punic Wars (264-146 BCE) present a monumental clash between Rome and Carthage, driven by competition for Mediterranean supremacy. The First Punic War saw naval engagements for control of Sicily, while Hannibal's audacious tactics during the Second Punic War, particularly the Battle of Cannae, demonstrated the potential of strategic genius against overwhelming odds. The eventual destruction of Carthage in the Third Punic War not only secured Rome's dominance but also marked the transformation of Rome into a powerful empire, setting the stage for its expansion across Europe.

The Mongol Conquests (1206-1368 CE) under Genghis Khan illustrate the rise of a formidable empire that unified the Mongol tribes and expanded across Asia and into Europe. The Mongols' military prowess led to the conquest of China and significant incursions into the Islamic world, culminating in the fall of Baghdad. Their invasions reshaped trade routes, especially the Silk Road, and left a lasting legacy on the territories they conquered, influencing cultural exchanges and political structures across Eurasia.

The Hundred Years' War (1337-1453) between England and France epitomizes the complexities of dynastic and territorial disputes. This protracted conflict transformed military tactics with battles like Crecy and Poitiers and saw the emergence of iconic figures such as Joan of Arc, symbolizing national identity and resistance. The war's conclusion not only altered the political landscape of France and England but also laid the groundwork for future nation-states.

The Thirty Years' War (1618-1648) represents one of the most destructive conflicts in European history, driven by religious and political strife. The war involved multiple powers, including France, Spain, and Sweden, and concluded with the Peace of Westphalia, which significantly impacted European politics and marked the beginning of state sovereignty as a foundational principle.

The Napoleonic Wars (1803-1815) highlight the rise and fall of Napoleon Bonaparte, whose military campaigns reshaped Europe. The wars showcased the impact of nationalism and modern warfare, leading to significant political changes, including the Congress of Vienna, which sought to restore order after decades of conflict.

The American Civil War (1861-1865) is a profound examination of internal conflict driven by issues of slavery and state rights. This war not only transformed the United States but also set the stage for a long and difficult Reconstruction Era, influencing civil rights movements in the years to come.

In the 20th century, World War I (1914-1918) and World War II (1939-1945) redefined global conflict on an unprecedented scale. WWI introduced trench warfare and technological advancements that changed military strategy, while WWII's total war approach and the Holocaust revealed the darkest aspects of humanity, leading to a reshaping of global power dynamics.

The Korean War (1950-1953) and the Vietnam War (1955-1975) exemplify Cold War tensions, with significant international involvement and lasting implications for U.S. foreign policy.

Finally, the Gulf War (1990-1991) and the War on Terror (2001-present) reflect modern warfare's complexities in the post-Cold War era, highlighting technological advancements and the evolving nature of international relations.

Through these conflicts, "The Biggest Wars in History" not only chronicles significant military engagements but also explores the enduring impact of war on societies, politics, and cultures worldwide, offering critical insights into the human condition and the relentless pursuit of peace.

Chapter 2

The Peloponnesian War

Origins of the Conflict
The Peloponnesian War, one of the most significant conflicts in ancient history, was rooted in the profound rivalry between two of the most powerful city-states of ancient Greece: Athens and Sparta. This rivalry was not merely a clash of military might but represented a fundamental conflict between two opposing ways of life, political systems, and cultural values.

Athens: The Epitome of Democracy and Naval Power
Athens, during the 5th century BCE, had evolved into a powerful democratic city-state renowned for its cultural achievements, naval prowess, and economic strength. The Athenian Empire, a result of its leadership in the Delian League, extended its influence across the Aegean Sea. This maritime dominance allowed Athens to control trade routes, accumulate wealth, and foster a vibrant intellectual and artistic culture. The democratic political system of Athens encouraged public participation in governance, promoting a sense of unity and collective identity among its citizens, which enhanced its resolve and ambition on the international stage.

Sparta: The Military Oligarchy
In stark contrast, Sparta was characterized by its militaristic and oligarchic society. Governed by a dual kingship and a council of elders, Spartan society was focused on discipline, austerity, and military training. From a young age, Spartan males were subjected to rigorous training in the agoge, developing them into formidable warriors. The Spartan economy relied heavily on agriculture and the subjugation of the Helots, a class of serfs who worked the land. The Spartan way of life prioritized collective strength over individual expression, creating a society that was deeply cohesive yet inflexible.

The Growing Tensions
The tensions between Athens and Sparta escalated as both sought to expand their influence throughout Greece. The immediate precursor to the Peloponnesian War was the increasing Athenian imperialism, which threatened the autonomy of other city-states, including those within the Peloponnesian League, led by Sparta. The relationship between these two city-states deteriorated over several years, marked by a series of disputes and skirmishes.

One significant flashpoint was the Athenian intervention in the affairs of the city-state of Potidaea, a member of the Peloponnesian League. Athens imposed economic sanctions and demanded Potidaea abandon its ties with Sparta, leading to hostility. The Spartan response was to rally its allies, including Corinth and Megara, who felt equally threatened by Athenian expansionism.

Additionally, the ideological divide between the two powers exacerbated hostilities. Sparta viewed Athenian democracy as a destabilizing force, while Athens regarded Sparta's oligarchic rule as archaic and oppressive. This mutual distrust was compounded by both powers' desire for hegemony in the Greek world.

The Outbreak of War
As diplomatic negotiations failed and tensions reached a boiling point, the Peloponnesian War broke out in 431 BCE. The initial phase of the conflict saw Athens adopt a defensive strategy, leveraging its naval strength to conduct raids against the Peloponnesian coast, while Sparta relied on its formidable land army to invade Athenian territory.

The Peloponnesian War was not just a military confrontation; it was an ideological struggle that encapsulated the very essence of Greek civilization at the time. The conflict would ultimately reshape the power dynamics of the ancient world, illustrating how the rivalry between Athens and Sparta was rooted in deep-seated differences that transcended mere territorial ambitions and reflected broader societal values and beliefs. Thus, the origins of the conflict were as much about culture and identity as they were about power and control, setting the stage for one of history's most pivotal wars.

Key Battles and Strategies of the Peloponnesian War
The Peloponnesian War, fought between 431 and 404 BCE, was a protracted and complex conflict primarily between two powerful city-states of ancient Greece: Athens and Sparta. The war is notable not only for its duration and the scale of its battles but also for the diverse military strategies employed by both sides. The following exploration highlights key battles and the strategies that shaped the course of the war.

The Archidamian War (431-421 BCE)
The initial phase of the Peloponnesian War, known as the Archidamian War, was characterized by a war of attrition. A prominent strategy employed by Sparta was the annual invasions of Attica, which was the region surrounding Athens. Led by King Archidamus II, Spartan forces would invade Athenian territory, destroying crops and property in a bid to weaken Athens economically and demoralize its populace. However, the Athenian strategy was markedly

different. Under the leadership of Pericles, Athens relied on its formidable navy and a defensive strategy that took advantage of its walls. Rather than engage directly in land battles, Athenians would retreat behind their city walls, relying on naval superiority to supply the city and conduct raids along the Peloponnesian coast.

The Battle of Pylos (425 BCE)
A significant turning point in the Archidamian War was the Battle of Pylos. Athenian forces, led by the general Cleon, captured the Spartan-held island of Pylos, which was strategically located near the Peloponnesian coast. This victory not only showcased the effectiveness of Athenian naval tactics but also led to the capture of Spartan hoplites on the nearby island of Sphacteria. The Athenians utilized their naval power to blockade the Spartans and effectively neutralized their forces, leading to a rare and significant Athenian triumph. This battle highlighted the strategic importance of naval power in the war and demonstrated the potential for Athenian innovation in military tactics.

The Sicilian Expedition (415-413 BCE)
Another pivotal moment in the war was the Sicilian Expedition, launched by Athens in 415 BCE. The objective was to conquer Sicily, which was seen as a rich and strategically vital region. The Athenian fleet, boasting a large number of ships and a considerable force, aimed to secure vital resources and expand Athenian influence. However, the expedition was marked by poor strategic planning and overambition. The Athenians faced stiff resistance from the Sicilian city-states and ultimately encountered a devastating defeat at the Battle of Syracuse. The loss decimated the Athenian navy and significantly weakened its military position, demonstrating the pitfalls of overextending military campaigns without adequate intelligence and support.

The Ionian or Decelean War (413-404 BCE)
The final phase of the Peloponnesian War, known as the Ionian War, saw a shift in strategies as both sides adapted to the realities of war. Sparta, with Persian financial support, expanded its naval capabilities, enabling it to challenge Athenian dominance at sea. The Battle of Aegospotami in 405 BCE marked the culmination of this phase, with Spartan forces decisively defeating the Athenian fleet. The battle was strategically significant as it cut off Athens from its crucial supply lines, leading to the eventual siege of Athens itself.

Conclusion
The Peloponnesian War serves as a profound study of military strategy and the interplay between land and naval forces. The contrasting approaches of Athens and Sparta—one emphasizing naval strength and the other land-based dominance—defined the conflict and influenced the outcomes of key battles. The war's strategies not only highlight the tactical

ingenuity of the ancient Greeks but also underscore the critical importance of adaptability in warfare. The lessons drawn from these battles continue to resonate in military theory and history today.

The Role of Leadership

Leadership plays a crucial role in the course and outcome of wars, shaping strategies, morale, and the very fabric of alliances and enmities. In the context of the Peloponnesian War, two leaders stand out: Pericles of Athens and Lysander of Sparta. Their contrasting leadership styles, strategic decisions, and personal charisma significantly influenced the trajectory of the conflict and ultimately determined the fate of their respective city-states.

Pericles: The Architect of Athenian Strategy

Pericles was a prominent statesman and general in Athens during the early years of the Peloponnesian War. His leadership was characterized by a vision of a strong, democratic Athens that could maintain its empire through naval superiority and strategic defense. Pericles believed in the importance of avoiding land battles with the superior Spartan army and instead advocated for a defensive strategy that leveraged Athens' naval power.

Under Pericles' guidance, Athens focused on consolidating its resources, fortifying its city walls, and utilizing its navy to conduct raids against the Peloponnesian coast. His famous strategy included encouraging the population of Attica to retreat behind the city walls, thus protecting them from Spartan invasion while relying on the fleet to supply the city and conduct offensive operations at sea.

Pericles' leadership also emphasized the importance of democracy and civic participation, rallying the Athenian populace around the war effort. His famous Funeral Oration, delivered after the first significant losses in the war, underscored Athenian values and the sacrifices made for the greater good, boosting morale and reinforcing commitment to the cause. However, his strategy faced significant challenges, particularly during the plague that struck Athens in 430 BCE, leading to devastating losses and widespread demoralization.

Lysander: The Spartan Commander

In contrast to Pericles, Lysander emerged as a key military leader for Sparta later in the war, particularly during its resurgence. A brilliant strategist, Lysander recognized the need to adapt Spartan methods to counter Athenian naval power. He formed alliances with Persia, securing the financial resources necessary to build a formidable fleet capable of challenging Athenian dominance at sea.

Lysander's leadership style was marked by decisiveness and a willingness to innovate. He understood that to defeat Athens, he needed to strike at its vulnerable points. His tactics included luring the Athenian fleet into traps and exploiting their weaknesses through superior knowledge of the terrain and naval tactics. The decisive victory at the Battle of Aegospotami in 405 BCE, where Lysander's forces effectively destroyed the Athenian fleet, was a pivotal moment in the war. This victory not only crippled Athenian naval power but also facilitated the siege of Athens, leading to the eventual surrender of the city in 404 BCE.

Contrasting Outcomes
The contrasting outcomes of Pericles and Lysander's leadership illustrate the profound impact that individual leaders can have on the course of history. Pericles' vision and strategies initially positioned Athens as the dominant power in the Greek world, but his inability to adapt to unforeseen challenges, such as the plague and the protracted nature of the war, ultimately undermined his legacy. Conversely, Lysander's ability to innovate and leverage external alliances contributed to Sparta's eventual victory, proving that effective leadership can pivot the tide of war even in the face of overwhelming odds.

In conclusion, the leadership of Pericles and Lysander during the Peloponnesian War exemplifies how individual leaders can shape the strategies, morale, and ultimate outcomes of conflicts. Their decisions, personalities, and adaptability not only influenced the war's progress but also left lasting legacies that would inform military and political thought for generations to come.

The War's Aftermath

The conclusion of the Peloponnesian War in 404 BCE marked a significant turning point in ancient Greek history, profoundly reshaping the political landscape of the region and leading to the decline of Athenian power. The conflict, primarily fought between two leading city-states, Athens and Sparta, not only decimated their military strength but also had far-reaching consequences for the entire Greek world.

One of the most immediate outcomes was the fall of Athens. After a protracted struggle characterized by shifting alliances and devastating battles, the Athenian navy was decisively defeated at Aegospotami. This loss culminated in a blockade of the Athenian port of Piraeus, leading to starvation and eventual surrender. The defeat had a catastrophic impact on Athens, which had been the cultural and intellectual hub of Greece. The once-mighty city fell under Spartan hegemony, and its walls were torn down, its fleet dismantled, and its empire stripped away. The imposition of an oligarchic government known as the "Thirty Tyrants" further exacerbated the city's turmoil, leading to internal strife and civil discord.

The Peloponnesian War also significantly altered the balance of power in Greece. With Athens weakened, Sparta emerged as the dominant power in the region. However, Spartan dominance was short-lived and marked by its inability to maintain control over a fragmented Greece. The hegemony of Sparta ushered in a period of instability characterized by social unrest and revolts among the subjugated city-states. The harsh treatment of previously allied states fostered resentment and resistance, which would later contribute to Spartan vulnerabilities.

In the aftermath of the war, the concept of city-state autonomy also underwent transformation. The war highlighted the fragility of alliances and the destructive potential of internecine conflict, leading many Greek city-states to reconsider their diplomatic strategies. The former allies of Athens sought new partnerships for protection and economic stability, while others, disillusioned by the prolonged violence, began to pursue neutrality.

Moreover, the war's impact extended beyond immediate military and political changes; it ushered in a profound cultural and intellectual shift. The war's devastation prompted philosophers and historians, like Thucydides, to reflect on the nature of power, justice, and human behavior. His work, "History of the Peloponnesian War," not only chronicled the events of the conflict but also laid the groundwork for a more critical approach to historical documentation and analysis, emphasizing the moral complexities and consequences of war. This shift in perspective would influence subsequent generations of thought, shaping the philosophical discourse surrounding ethics in governance and warfare.

The decline of Athenian power also created a vacuum that would eventually enable the rise of Macedon under Philip II and his son, Alexander the Great. The weakened state of the Greek city-states made them susceptible to external conquest, fundamentally altering the course of Greek history. Alexander's conquests would lead to the Hellenistic period, characterized by the spread of Greek culture across a vast empire but at the cost of the independent city-states that had once thrived.

In conclusion, the aftermath of the Peloponnesian War reshaped the Greek world in profound ways, leading to the decline of Athenian power and altering the political landscape of the region. The war's consequences prompted a reevaluation of alliances and governance, spurred significant cultural reflections on human nature and conflict, and ultimately paved the way for the rise of new powers in a fragmented Greece. The lessons learned from this tumultuous period would resonate throughout history, influencing not just the Greeks but civilizations beyond.

The Legacy of the Peloponnesian War

The Peloponnesian War (431-404 BCE), fought between the city-states of Athens and Sparta, stands as one of the most significant conflicts in ancient history. Its ramifications extended far beyond the immediate military and political outcomes, influencing subsequent generations' military strategies, political philosophies, and the broader understanding of war itself.

Military Thought and Strategy
The Peloponnesian War introduced a variety of military strategies that would shape future conflicts. Thucydides, the war's chronicler, provided insights into the strategic thinking of leaders like Pericles and Alcibiades. A key aspect of Athenian strategy was its reliance on naval power and the use of the long walls, which connected Athens to its port, Piraeus. This infrastructure enabled the Athenians to maintain supply lines and project power across the Aegean Sea. The war highlighted the significance of maritime strategy, which would influence later naval doctrines, particularly during the rise of empires such as Rome and, later, Great Britain.

Sparta's strategy, on the other hand, emphasized land power, disciplined hoplite warfare, and the importance of alliances. The conflict illustrated the effectiveness of combined arms tactics, where infantry and cavalry worked in concert, an approach that would resonate through military literature and practice in centuries to come. The use of deception and psychological warfare, as seen in the Sicilian Expedition, also foreshadowed tactics employed in later conflicts.

Political Philosophy
Politically, the Peloponnesian War profoundly influenced thinkers such as Plato and Aristotle, who grappled with the implications of the war on governance and ethics. The war's devastation led to a reevaluation of democracy, particularly in Athens, where the radicalism that characterized its democratic processes was both praised and criticized. The rise and fall of political factions during the war offered a real-world case study of the fragility of democratic systems, leading to philosophical inquiries about the nature of power, justice, and the role of the citizenry in governance.

Thucydides himself, through his historical narrative, posited that human nature, driven by fear, self-interest, and honor, was a constant in political life. His reflections on realpolitik, particularly in the Melian Dialogue, which rationalizes power politics and the inevitability of conflict, paved the way for future political theorists, including Machiavelli and Hobbes, who would later explore similar themes of power, morality, and statecraft.

Cultural Impact

The Peloponnesian War also left an indelible mark on literature and culture. Its depiction of the tragic consequences of hubris, civil strife, and the moral ambiguities of war resonated through works of literature, inspiring writers and historians for centuries. The themes of loyalty, betrayal, and the human cost of conflict became central to Western literature, influencing playwrights such as Euripides and Sophocles, who examined the psychological and societal repercussions of war within their tragedies.

The war's legacy can also be seen in the broader discourse on peace and conflict resolution. The eventual Spartan victory and the subsequent imposition of oligarchic rule in Athens led to a period of instability and reflection on the nature of power and governance, thus sowing the seeds for future philosophical discussions on the balance of power and the need for checks and balances in governance.

Conclusion

In sum, the Peloponnesian War served as a crucible of military strategy, political philosophy, and cultural expression. Its multifaceted legacy continues to inform contemporary understandings of warfare, governance, and human nature. As both a cautionary tale and a source of inspiration, the conflict invites ongoing reflection on the complexities of human society and the perennial challenges of achieving lasting peace in a world often beset by strife.

Chapter 3

The Punic Wars

Rome vs. Carthage

The Punic Wars, a series of three significant conflicts fought between Rome and Carthage from 264 BCE to 146 BCE, marked a pivotal turning point in the ancient Mediterranean world. These wars not only determined the fate of two powerful city-states but also reshaped the balance of power across the Mediterranean region. Understanding the origins and causes of the Punic Wars requires a look at the geographical, political, and economic factors that fueled the rivalry between these two formidable powers.

Carthage, located in present-day Tunisia, was originally a Phoenician colony and had evolved into a dominant maritime power by the 3rd century BCE. Its strategic position allowed it to control trade routes across the western Mediterranean and establish a vast network of colonies and trading posts, particularly in North Africa, Sicily, and parts of Spain. The wealth generated from this trade enabled Carthage to build a formidable navy and maintain a strong military presence, which posed a threat to other regional powers, most notably Rome.

Rome, on the other hand, was a burgeoning land power with ambitions of expansion. By the mid-3rd century BCE, it had successfully unified much of the Italian peninsula and was seeking to extend its influence beyond its borders. The competition for control over Sicily, a crucial trading hub located between the two powers, served as the flashpoint for conflict. The island was not only strategically significant for trade but also held agricultural importance that both Rome and Carthage coveted.

The immediate cause of the First Punic War (264-241 BCE) arose from a dispute over the control of Sicily, particularly the city of Messana. When the Mamertines, a group of mercenaries who had seized Messana, sought assistance from both Rome and Carthage, it set off a chain reaction. Rome's decision to intervene militarily was motivated by a desire to prevent Carthage from expanding its influence in a territory that Rome considered vital to its interests. This intervention escalated into a full-blown conflict, leading to a protracted struggle that highlighted both powers' military capabilities and strategic ambitions.

Underlying the immediate causes of the Punic Wars were deeper-seated issues related to economic competition and imperial aspirations. Carthage's wealth derived from its extensive trade networks, while Rome's strength was based on its land conquests and agricultural production. The competition for resources and trade routes fueled animosity and suspicion between the two powers, with each side viewing the other as a formidable rival. Furthermore, as Rome expanded its territory and influence, it increasingly came into conflict with Carthage's interests, creating a zero-sum game where one power's gain was perceived as the other's loss.

The Punic Wars were also shaped by the contrasting political systems of the two states. Rome's republican governance allowed for a more flexible and responsive military strategy, while Carthage's oligarchic system often led to internal discord and inefficiency in decision-making. This disparity in political structures affected how each state mobilized resources and adapted to the changing dynamics of warfare.

Ultimately, the Punic Wars were not merely a struggle for territorial dominance; they were emblematic of the larger contest for supremacy in the Mediterranean. The conflict between Rome and Carthage encapsulated the themes of ambition, rivalry, and the quest for power that defined the ancient world. The outcomes of these wars would shape the future of Rome, leading it to emerge as a dominant empire while marking the decline of Carthage as a significant power in the region. Thus, the origins and causes of the Punic Wars reflect a complex interplay of strategic interests, economic competition, and political dynamics that set the stage for one of history's most consequential military confrontations.

The First Punic War

The First Punic War (264–241 BCE) marked a pivotal moment in the ancient world, as it set the stage for the long-standing rivalry between two of the Mediterranean's dominant powers: Rome and Carthage. The war was primarily fought over control of Sicily, an island of strategic importance that served as a critical point of trade and military operations in the region. The conflict arose from a complex interplay of economic interests, regional dominance, and burgeoning national pride, ultimately leading to a series of naval battles that would redefine the nature of warfare in the Mediterranean.

Carthage, a Phoenician city-state located in present-day Tunisia, had established itself as a formidable maritime power, boasting a well-trained navy and extensive trade networks across the Mediterranean. In contrast, Rome was primarily a land-based power, with little experience in naval warfare. The initial catalyst for the war was the dispute over the city of Messana in northeastern Sicily, where both powers sought to exert influence. The situation escalated when the Mamertines, a group of mercenaries who had seized Messana, appealed to both Rome and Carthage for assistance.

In 264 BCE, Rome responded by sending troops to Messana, igniting hostilities with Carthage, which saw the Roman presence as a direct threat to its interests in Sicily. The war quickly transitioned from a territorial dispute to a larger conflict that would see both powers vying for control of the island.

The First Punic War was characterized by significant naval engagements, as control of the seas was critical to securing supply lines and troop movements. The Romans, recognizing their lack of naval experience, embarked on an ambitious program to build a fleet capable of challenging Carthage at sea. They developed the corvus, a boarding device that allowed Roman soldiers to engage enemy ships in hand-to-hand combat, effectively neutralizing Carthage's superior seamanship.

One of the first major naval battles occurred at Mylae in 260 BCE, where the Roman fleet, under the command of Gaius Duilius, achieved a decisive victory against the Carthaginian navy. This battle was significant not only for its immediate tactical success but also for its psychological impact, as it marked Rome's emergence as a formidable naval power. The victory at Mylae was followed by further naval engagements, including the Battle of Ecnomus in 256 BCE, where the Romans again bested the Carthaginians, solidifying their control over the western Mediterranean.

Despite these successes, the nature of warfare during the First Punic War was marked by a series of challenges for both sides. Carthage, although initially dominant at sea, struggled to maintain its supply lines and troop morale, particularly as the war dragged on. The Romans, meanwhile, faced logistical difficulties and the need to adapt rapidly to the naval warfare environment, leading to both successes and setbacks.

As the war progressed, the focus shifted to land battles in Sicily, with both powers vying for key cities. The Romans launched several campaigns, gradually capturing strategic locations, including Lilybaeum and Lilybaeum's port, which became crucial for their operations. The protracted conflict and the increasing strain on both economies eventually pushed Carthage to the brink, leading to a depletion of resources and public support for the war.

The First Punic War concluded in 241 BCE with the Treaty of Lutatius, which imposed significant reparations on Carthage and ceded control of Sicily to Rome. This conflict not only marked the beginning of Roman expansion beyond the Italian peninsula but also laid the groundwork for future confrontations, notably the Second Punic War. The First Punic War ultimately transformed the balance of power in the Mediterranean, establishing Rome as a preeminent naval force and shaping the trajectory of Western history.

The Second Punic War

The Second Punic War (218-201 BCE) was one of the most significant and pivotal conflicts in ancient history, marked by the extraordinary military campaigns of the Carthaginian general Hannibal Barca. This war was primarily a struggle for dominance in the Mediterranean, ignited by the long-standing rivalry between Rome and Carthage. While the war encompassed numerous battles and strategies, Hannibal's audacious invasion of Italy and the subsequent Battle of Cannae stand out as defining moments that showcased his military genius and the grave threat he posed to Rome.

Hannibal's invasion of Italy began with his daring crossing of the Alps in 218 BCE, a maneuver that would become legendary. He led a diverse army, comprising infantry, cavalry, and war elephants, through treacherous mountain passes. This unexpected approach caught the Romans off guard and allowed Hannibal to enter the Italian Peninsula. His strategy was not merely to engage in direct confrontation; rather, he aimed to undermine Roman morale and encourage their allies to defect. As he swept through Northern Italy, Hannibal achieved a series of victories against Roman forces, including the battles at the Trebia River and Lake Trasimene, which further established his reputation as a formidable commander.

The Battle of Cannae, fought on August 2, 216 BCE, would become the pinnacle of Hannibal's military career and a classic study in battlefield tactics. The Romans, under the command of two consuls, Lucius Emilius Paullus and Gaius Terentius Varro, assembled one of the largest armies in their history, numbering approximately 86,000 men. In contrast, Hannibal commanded around 50,000 troops, a mixture of his seasoned North African soldiers and Gallic allies. Despite being outnumbered, Hannibal's tactical acumen set the stage for one of the most devastating defeats in Roman history.

Hannibal employed a double-envelopment tactic at Cannae, a maneuver that would become a hallmark of military strategy. He positioned his troops in a crescent shape, allowing the Roman forces to push forward and become overextended. As the Romans pressed into the center, Hannibal's troops gradually closed in from the flanks. The resulting encirclement trapped the Roman legions, leading to chaos and panic. The Romans suffered catastrophic losses, with estimates of casualties ranging from 50,000 to 70,000 soldiers, while Hannibal's forces incurred far fewer losses.

The aftermath of Cannae had profound implications for Rome and the course of the Second Punic War. The defeat shocked the Roman Republic to its core, causing widespread fear and prompting several of Rome's allies to reconsider their allegiances. However, rather than capitalizing on his victory by marching on Rome, Hannibal chose a more cautious approach, opting to consolidate his control of Southern Italy and seeking to win over local populations.

In the wake of Cannae, Rome's response was characterized by resilience and strategic adaptability. Under the leadership of figures like Publius Cornelius Scipio, the Romans shifted their military tactics, avoiding large-scale confrontations with Hannibal's forces and instead focusing on attrition and counter-offensives. This eventually set the stage for Rome's resurgence, culminating in Scipio's decisive victory at the Battle of Zama in 202 BCE, which ultimately led to the end of the Second Punic War.

Hannibal's invasion of Italy and the Battle of Cannae remain emblematic of the complexities of warfare, showcasing the interplay of strategy, leadership, and the unpredictable nature of conflict. Hannibal's legacy as one of history's greatest military leaders endures, illustrating the lasting impact that a single conflict can have on the evolution of warfare and the fate of empires.

The Third Punic War and the Destruction of Carthage

The Third Punic War (149–146 BCE) marked the final chapter in the protracted conflict between Rome and Carthage, two of the most powerful entities in the ancient Mediterranean. This war was not merely a military engagement but a culmination of deep-seated animosities, political maneuvering, and the inexorable expansion of Roman imperial ambitions. The outcome of this war not only resulted in the total destruction of Carthage but also solidified Roman dominance over the Mediterranean basin, laying the groundwork for the establishment of one of history's most influential empires.

The origins of the Third Punic War are rooted in the aftermath of the previous Punic Wars, particularly the Second Punic War (218–201 BCE), where Rome had emerged victorious but not without significant cost. Despite its defeat, Carthage had managed to recover economically and politically, leading to growing fears in Rome. The Roman senator Cato the Elder famously ended his speeches with the phrase "Carthago delenda est" ("Carthage must be destroyed"), encapsulating the prevailing sentiment that Carthage was a persistent threat to Roman security and dominance.

Tensions escalated when Carthage, against the terms of its treaty with Rome, engaged in military actions against its neighbor, Numidia. Rome, citing self-defense and preemptive security, declared war on Carthage. However, the conflict was less about immediate threats than it was about the broader objective of extinguishing Carthage as a rival power. The Romans employed a combination of military might and psychological warfare, facing a Carthaginian populace that was initially reluctant to fight but gradually rallied under the leadership of figures like Hasdrubal.

The Roman campaign was marked by a series of strategic decisions that showcased Roman military prowess. The siege of Carthage, which began in 149 BCE, was a protracted affair that demonstrated Rome's determination and engineering capabilities. The Romans constructed a formidable blockade, cutting off Carthage from reinforcements and supplies, while employing siege tactics that included constructing walls and fortifications to encircle the city.

The climax of the Third Punic War came in 146 BCE, when Roman forces, led by General Scipio Aemilianus, launched a full-scale assault on the city. After a brutal and bloody siege that lasted for three years, the Romans breached Carthage's defenses. What followed was a systematic campaign of destruction; the city was razed, and its inhabitants either killed or sold into slavery. The fall of Carthage was not merely a military victory but a symbolic act of obliteration, reflecting Rome's desire to eradicate the memory of a rival that had once threatened its hegemony.

The destruction of Carthage had profound implications for the Mediterranean world. With Carthage eliminated, Rome secured its position as the preeminent power in the region. The vast territories previously under Carthaginian control, including parts of North Africa and Spain, came under Roman dominion, allowing for greater economic exploitation and the establishment of Roman colonies. This expansion facilitated trade routes and the integration of diverse cultures into the Roman Empire, paving the way for a period of relative peace known as the Pax Romana.

Moreover, the annihilation of Carthage served as a stark warning to other states about the consequences of opposing Rome. The phrase "Carthago delenda est" became a rallying cry for Roman expansionism, reinforcing the idea that Rome would not tolerate any threats to its supremacy. The Third Punic War thus did not only mark the end of Carthage but also heralded the beginning of an era of Roman dominance that would shape the course of Mediterranean and world history for centuries to come.

The Impact of the Punic Wars

The Punic Wars, fought between Rome and Carthage from 264 BC to 146 BC, were monumental in transforming Rome from a regional power into a dominant Mediterranean empire. This series of conflicts not only established Rome's military prowess but also had profound implications for its political structure, economy, and culture, laying the groundwork for centuries of Roman dominance.

At the outset of the First Punic War, Rome was primarily a land-based power with a focus on expanding its influence within the Italian peninsula. However, the war marked a significant shift as Rome engaged in naval warfare to secure control over Sicily, a crucial trade route and strategic location. The construction of a formidable navy, despite Rome's initial inexperience at sea, showcased the adaptability and resourcefulness of the Roman state. Victory in the First Punic War (241 BC) not only afforded Rome its first overseas territory but also emphasized its commitment to maritime power, a precursor to its later dominance over the Mediterranean.

The Second Punic War (218-201 BC) further solidified Rome's status as a military superpower. Hannibal's audacious invasion of Italy, characterized by his strategic brilliance and the crossing of the Alps, posed a significant threat to Roman supremacy. However, the Roman response, particularly the innovative tactics employed by generals such as Scipio Africanus, led to decisive victories, most notably at the Battle of Zama in 202 BC. This conflict marked the end of Carthage as a significant rival and allowed Rome to establish itself as the uncontested power in the western Mediterranean.

The consequences of these wars extended beyond mere territorial gains. The acquisition of vast resources and wealth from conquered lands fueled Rome's economy, resulting in increased trade and commerce. The annexation of territories such as Sicily, Sardinia, and parts of North Africa provided Rome with access to critical agricultural products and raw materials, transforming its economy and elevating its status among Mediterranean powers.

Politically, the Punic Wars instigated changes within Roman governance. The expansion of territory necessitated a more complex administrative structure, leading to the establishment of provinces governed by Roman officials. This system not only facilitated the management of Rome's vast empire but also allowed for the dissemination of Roman culture and law, which became integral to the identity of the empire. The influx of wealth and resources also intensified social stratification and contributed to tensions between the patricians and plebeians in Rome, setting the stage for future conflicts, including the Gracchi reforms and the eventual transition to imperial rule.

Culturally, the Punic Wars stimulated a sense of Roman identity and exceptionalism. The narrative of victory over a formidable opponent like Carthage became a source of pride and a foundational myth for Roman society. This sense of identity was further bolstered by the emergence of literature and historical accounts that celebrated Roman valor and military achievements, such as those by historians like Polybius and Livy. Such cultural developments fostered a unified Roman identity that transcended regional differences, crucial for maintaining cohesion in an expanding empire.

In conclusion, the Punic Wars were instrumental in transforming Rome into a powerful empire. They not only facilitated territorial expansion and economic prosperity but also prompted significant political and cultural shifts. As Rome emerged from these conflicts, it laid the groundwork for its future expansion, ultimately paving the way for the establishment of one of history's most influential empires. The legacy of the Punic Wars continues to resonate, illustrating the complexities of war and its transformative power on societies and civilizations throughout history.

Chapter 4

The Mongol Conquests

Genghis Khan and the Rise of the Mongol Empire

Genghis Khan, born as Temujin around 1162, emerged from the harsh and unforgiving steppes of Mongolia. His early life was marked by hardship; he was the son of a tribal chief who was poisoned by rivals, leaving Temujin and his family vulnerable to attack and destitution. This difficult upbringing instilled in him a profound understanding of the need for unity and strength among the disparate Mongol tribes, which were often embroiled in internal conflicts.

By the late 12th century, Mongolia was a patchwork of tribes and clans, each vying for power and resources. The Mongol tribes were characterized by their nomadic lifestyle, moving with their herds of horses, sheep, and goats. They were skilled horsemen and archers, traits that would later prove crucial in warfare. However, their lack of unity made them vulnerable to external threats and internal strife. Temujin recognized that to survive and thrive, the tribes would need to unite under a single banner.

In the 1180s, Temujin began his campaign for unification. He employed a combination of diplomacy, strategic marriages, and military prowess to consolidate power. One of his first significant alliances was with the Onggirat tribe, which provided him with crucial support. He also married Börte, who became a key ally in his rise to power, further solidifying his position among the tribes. Temujin's exceptional leadership skills and charisma attracted followers, and he began to forge a coalition that transcended tribal affiliations.

The turning point in Temujin's quest for unification came during the Battle of Dalan Baljut in 1187, where he successfully defeated the Tayichi'ud, a powerful rival tribe. This victory established his reputation as a formidable leader and allowed him to gather more support from other tribes. Temujin's approach was revolutionary for the time; he promoted individuals based on merit rather than noble birth, which appealed to many warriors who had previously been marginalized. This meritocratic system fostered loyalty and encouraged talented individuals to join his ranks, thereby strengthening his military capabilities.

By 1206, after years of warfare and negotiation, Temujin had achieved a remarkable feat: he unified the Mongol tribes and was proclaimed Genghis Khan, which translates to "universal ruler." This title signified not only the unification of the Mongols but also the beginning of a transformative era in world history. Under his leadership, the Mongols adopted a more organized military structure, utilizing superior cavalry tactics, mobility, and psychological warfare, which would become hallmarks of their campaigns.

With the Mongol tribes united, Genghis Khan set his sights beyond the steppes. His first major conquest was against the Khwarezmian Empire in 1219, a powerful state that spanned parts of present-day Iran, Uzbekistan, and Kazakhstan. The initial diplomatic overtures were met with treachery, prompting Genghis Khan to unleash his armies. The Mongols employed swift and brutal tactics, utilizing their mastery of cavalry and archery to devastating effect. The conquests that followed not only expanded the Mongol Empire into one of the largest contiguous empires in history but also established trade routes and cultural exchanges that would shape Eurasian history.

In conclusion, Genghis Khan's unification of the Mongol tribes and subsequent conquests laid the groundwork for an empire that would stretch from Eastern Europe to the Sea of Japan. His innovative military strategies, emphasis on meritocracy, and diplomatic acumen were pivotal in his rise, marking the beginning of the Mongol Empire's profound impact on world history. Through his leadership, Genghis Khan not only transformed the Mongolian landscape but also reshaped the dynamics of power across continents.

The Conquest of China

The Mongol Conquest of China, primarily during the 13th century, stands as a pivotal chapter in the history of both China and the Mongol Empire. The Mongols, under the leadership of Genghis Khan and his successors, embarked on a campaign that would ultimately lead to the establishment of the Yuan Dynasty in China. This conquest was characterized by a series of strategic military engagements, psychological warfare, and the exploitation of existing political divisions within China.

The Initial Campaigns Against the Jin Dynasty

The first significant phase of the Mongol invasion of China targeted the Jin Dynasty, which ruled over northern China. The Jin had previously defeated the Northern Song Dynasty, thus holding significant power and territory. Genghis Khan initiated his campaign against the Jin around 1211, capitalizing on the Jin's weakened state due to internal strife and external pressures.

The Mongols employed highly mobile cavalry units, known for their exceptional horsemanship and archery skills. This mobility allowed them to execute rapid raids into Jin territory. In 1215, the Mongols laid siege to the Jin capital of Zhongdu (modern-day Beijing). Utilizing siege technologies acquired from various cultures, including Chinese engineers who were captured, the Mongols were able to breach the walls of the city. The fall of Zhongdu was a significant blow to the Jin Dynasty, leading to a series of defeats that culminated in the complete collapse of Jin rule by 1234.

The Campaign Against the Song Dynasty
After the conquest of the Jin Dynasty, the Mongols turned their attention southward to the Song Dynasty, which controlled southern China. The Song Dynasty was known for its economic prosperity and cultural achievements but was politically fragmented and militarily less robust compared to the Jin. This division would prove advantageous for the Mongols.

The Mongol campaigns against the Song began in earnest under the leadership of Kublai Khan, the grandson of Genghis Khan. The Mongols employed tactics that included dividing and conquering, using local alliances to undermine Song defenses. The Mongols capitalized on the Song's reliance on fortified cities, which were often besieged through coordinated assaults and psychological tactics designed to instill fear among the defenders.

Key Battles and Strategies
The most notable battle in the conquest of the Song was the siege of Xiangyang (1267-1273). This city was strategically located and well-fortified, serving as a gateway to southern China. The Mongols, applying advanced siege technologies and persistent warfare, eventually breached Xiangyang's defenses, opening the door for a further advance into the heart of Song territory.

Kublai Khan also recognized the importance of controlling supply lines and trade routes, which the Song heavily relied upon. By disrupting these lines, the Mongols weakened Song military capabilities and morale. The Mongol strategy of employing local knowledge and engineers allowed them to adapt to the sophisticated fortifications of the Song.

The Fall of the Song Dynasty
By 1279, the Mongols had achieved a decisive victory at the naval battle of Yamen, where the combined forces of the Song were defeated. With the fall of the Song Dynasty, Kublai Khan declared the establishment of the Yuan Dynasty, marking the first time in over a millennium that China was united under foreign rule.

Conclusion
The Mongol conquest of China was not merely a military endeavor; it was a complex interplay of strategy, psychology, and the exploitation of existing political vulnerabilities. The rapid Mongol advances showcased their military prowess, but it also highlighted the divisions within Chinese

dynasties that ultimately facilitated their conquest. This period laid the foundation for significant changes in Chinese society, culture, and governance, the repercussions of which would resonate throughout history. The Mongols not only reshaped the political landscape of China but also influenced trade, culture, and technology across Eurasia, marking a transformative era in world history.

The Invasion of the Islamic World

The invasion of the Islamic world during the 13th century, particularly marked by the Mongol conquest of Baghdad in 1258, represents a significant turning point in both Islamic history and global civilization. This event not only led to the collapse of one of the most influential centers of learning and culture but also signaled the end of the Islamic Golden Age, a period characterized by remarkable advancements in science, philosophy, medicine, and the arts.

Baghdad, as the capital of the Abbasid Caliphate, was more than just a political center; it was a thriving hub of intellectual activity and cultural exchange. Scholars from various backgrounds, including Persian, Arab, Greek, and Indian, converged in the city, contributing to advancements in mathematics, astronomy, medicine, and philosophy. The House of Wisdom, established in Baghdad, was a pivotal institution where scholars translated and preserved ancient texts, and where innovations flourished. The city epitomized the spirit of inquiry and knowledge that marked the Islamic Golden Age, which spanned from the 8th to the 14th centuries.

The Mongol invasion, led by Hulagu Khan, was precipitated by a combination of military ambition and political intrigue. The Mongols, having unified under Genghis Khan and subsequently expanded across Asia, saw the rich territories of the Islamic world as ripe for conquest. Baghdad's strategic location along trade routes and its wealth made it a prime target. In February 1258, after laying siege to the city, the Mongols breached its defenses. The ensuing sacking of Baghdad was catastrophic; historical accounts describe widespread destruction, including the burning of libraries and the slaughter of thousands of inhabitants. Estimates suggest that the population of Baghdad, which had been around one million, dwindled drastically, with countless lives lost during the siege and its aftermath.

The fall of Baghdad had profound repercussions not only for the city but also for the Islamic world and beyond. The immediate impact was the disintegration of the Abbasid Caliphate's political authority, which had been a unifying force in the Islamic realm. The Mongols established a new regime, but their rule was often met with resistance and did not recover the cultural vibrancy of the previous era.

In the long term, the invasion disrupted the intellectual currents that had flourished under the Abbasids. Many scholars fled the region, scattering throughout the Islamic world and beyond, taking with them the knowledge they had accumulated. However, the loss of Baghdad as a cultural center stunted further advancements in science and philosophy. The invasion marked a shift in the Islamic world, where the focus shifted from scholarly pursuits to survival and resistance against foreign rule.

Moreover, the invasion of Baghdad signified a broader decline in the Islamic Golden Age. The political fragmentation that followed the Mongol conquest led to the rise of regional powers, each with its own interests and priorities, further diluting the coherence of Islamic scholarship and culture. While pockets of knowledge persisted in other cities like Cairo and Damascus, the collective intellectual momentum of the Golden Age was significantly diminished.

In summary, the Mongol invasion and the fall of Baghdad were pivotal events that not only marked the end of the Islamic Golden Age but also reshaped the trajectory of Islamic civilization. The destruction of Baghdad's cultural and intellectual legacy had lasting effects, leading to a period of stagnation that would take centuries to overcome. The invasion serves as a stark reminder of how warfare can obliterate centers of knowledge and culture, altering the course of history irrevocably.

The European Campaigns

The Mongol invasions of Eastern Europe during the 13th century marked a significant chapter in both European and Eurasian history, characterized by a series of military campaigns that left an indelible imprint on the landscape of the continent. Following the unification of the Mongol tribes under Genghis Khan, the Mongol Empire expanded rapidly, bringing vast territories under its control. By the time of Genghis Khan's death in 1227, the Mongols had already begun their incursions into Eastern Europe, which would culminate in a series of devastating campaigns led by his successors.

The first significant Mongol incursion into Europe occurred in 1241 during the reign of Batu Khan, a grandson of Genghis Khan. The Mongol forces, having already conquered much of Russia, turned their attention westward, launching a coordinated assault on Poland and Hungary. Key battles, such as the Battle of Legnica (1241) and the Battle of Mohi (1241), showcased the Mongols' tactical innovation and superior cavalry tactics. Utilizing their famed horse archers, the Mongols could maneuver swiftly on the battlefield, outflanking and overwhelming European forces, who were often unprepared for the ferocity and speed of the Mongol onslaught.

The Mongol campaigns in Eastern Europe also had profound political ramifications. The widespread devastation wrought by the Mongol armies led to significant destabilization in the region. Major cities such as Kiev were sacked, resulting in a power vacuum that allowed for the rise of new political entities. The fragmented political landscape of Eastern Europe, characterized by numerous feudal states, proved to be particularly vulnerable to Mongol tactics, which exploited local rivalries and divisions. This fragmentation set the stage for the eventual rise of centralized powers in the region, such as the Grand Duchy of Lithuania and the Kingdom of Poland, as local rulers sought to consolidate their power in the face of external threats.

The Mongol invasions also left a lasting influence on military strategies in Europe. The ferocity and effectiveness of the Mongol cavalry prompted European states to rethink their military organization and tactics. The need for rapid response forces and the integration of lighter cavalry units into existing armies became a topic of interest among European military leaders. Additionally, the psychological impact of the invasions fostered a sense of urgency regarding the fortification of cities and the establishment of more organized military coalitions among rival states.

Culturally, the Mongol invasions facilitated increased interactions between East and West. The Mongols established trade routes that connected Europe with Asia, leading to the exchange of ideas, technologies, and goods. This interaction would eventually contribute to the European Renaissance, as knowledge from the East began to filter into Western Europe through these channels. The Silk Road, while primarily known for its trade in silk and spices, also became a conduit for the transfer of military technologies and tactics, as well as philosophical and scientific ideas.

In summary, the Mongol invasions of Eastern Europe were not merely a series of military campaigns but rather a catalyst for significant political, military, and cultural transformations in the region. The devastation caused by the Mongols reshaped the political landscape, leading to the emergence of new powers and fostering military innovations that would influence European warfare for centuries to come. Furthermore, the increased interaction between East and West laid the groundwork for future exchanges that would enrich both regions, ultimately altering the course of European history. The legacy of the Mongol invasions serves as a poignant reminder of the profound impacts that conflicts can have on the evolution of societies and their interconnections.

The Legacy of the Mongol Empire

The Mongol Empire, which flourished in the 13th and 14th centuries under the leadership of Genghis Khan and his successors, was the largest contiguous empire in history. Its legacy is profound, shaping the geopolitical, cultural, and economic landscapes of Eurasia and profoundly influencing the course of world history.

One of the most significant impacts of the Mongol Empire was its role in facilitating trade and cultural exchange across vast distances, particularly along the Silk Road. The Mongols established a vast network of trade routes that connected the East and West, significantly enhancing commerce and communication between disparate regions. Under Mongol rule, merchants were granted protection and safe passage across the Empire, ensuring the security of trade caravans. This environment of safety encouraged the flow of goods, ideas, and technologies, leading to an unprecedented level of intercultural exchange. Spices, silks, precious metals, and other commodities traveled along these routes, while innovations such as papermaking and gunpowder made their way from one civilization to another, fundamentally altering the fabric of societies.

Furthermore, the Mongol Empire acted as a unifying force among diverse cultures and peoples. The Mongols promoted a policy of religious tolerance, allowing various faiths to coexist within their realm. As a result, the empire became a melting pot of cultures, where ideas from Buddhism, Islam, Christianity, and other belief systems intermingled. This openness not only fostered mutual understanding but also led to the sharing of artistic styles, scientific knowledge, and technological advancements. For example, the Persian miniature painting style was influenced by Chinese artistic traditions, while the spread of Persian literature influenced other cultures across the empire.

The Mongol Empire's administrative innovations also left a lasting legacy. The establishment of a postal system and relay stations (the Yam) enhanced communication across the empire, enabling messages and goods to traverse vast distances quickly. This infrastructure not only served military purposes but also facilitated trade and governance, creating a model for future empires. The Mongols' emphasis on meritocracy and the use of skilled administrators from various backgrounds helped shape bureaucratic practices in many regions, influencing governance in places like China and Persia long after the empire's decline.

Moreover, the Mongol Empire's impact on warfare and military strategy reverberated through history. The Mongols introduced new tactics, such as the use of mounted archers and psychological warfare, which would be adopted and adapted by future military leaders across the globe. Their emphasis on mobility and speed changed the nature of warfare, influencing military thinking in both the East and the West.

The decline of the Mongol Empire did not erase its influence; instead, it set the stage for the rise of successor states that inherited aspects of Mongol governance and culture. The Yuan Dynasty in China, for instance, continued to promote trade and cultural exchange, maintaining the infrastructure established during Mongol rule. In Russia, the Mongol period, known as the "Mongol Yoke," profoundly affected the development of Russian statehood and identity.

In conclusion, the legacy of the Mongol Empire is a testament to its transformative role in shaping Eurasian history. Through its facilitation of trade, cultural exchange, administrative innovations, and military strategies, the Mongol Empire not only connected diverse civilizations but also laid the groundwork for future developments in commerce, culture, and governance. The echoes of Mongol influence can still be felt in the modern world, reminding us of the interconnectedness of human societies throughout history.

Chapter 5

The Hundred Years' War

The Origins of the Conflict

The Hundred Years' War (1337-1453) between England and France was not a singular event but rather a series of conflicts rooted in deep-seated dynastic, territorial, and economic disputes. At its core, the war represented a struggle for power and influence, primarily over the French throne and the territories of France, particularly those regions held by the English crown.

Dynastic Disputes

The origins of the conflict can be traced back to the complex lineage of the French royal family. In the early 14th century, the French Capetian dynasty faced a succession crisis. After the death of Charles IV in 1328, the French crown passed to Philip VI of the Valois branch, which was contested by Edward III of England. Edward was the son of Isabella, the daughter of Philip IV of France. He claimed he had a legitimate right to the throne due to his maternal lineage. However, the French nobility favored Philip VI, leading to Edward's discontent and the assertion of his claim, which would ignite the conflict.

Territorial Disputes

In addition to dynastic issues, territorial disputes were a significant factor. The English crown possessed extensive territories in France due to earlier conquests and marriages. The most notable of these was the Duchy of Aquitaine, which was granted to the English king by the French crown. This arrangement created inevitable friction, as Philip VI sought to reassert control over these lands. Edward III's desire to maintain and expand his holdings, coupled with Philip VI's determination to reclaim territories, fueled tensions that would ultimately lead to war.

Economic Factors

Economic motivations also played a critical role in the origins of the Hundred Years' War. The region of Flanders, a wealthy area that depended heavily on the wool trade with England, became a focal point of conflict. English wool was vital for the Flemish textile industry, and the economic interdependence between England and Flanders complicated the political landscape. As the French monarchy sought to exert control over Flanders and curb English influence, it further exacerbated tensions between the two kingdoms. Consequently, Edward III allied himself with Flanders' leaders, who resisted French control, thereby broadening the conflict's dimensions.

The Initial Outbreak of War
The culmination of these dynastic claims, territorial ambitions, and economic interests led to the outbreak of hostilities in 1337. Philip VI confiscated the Duchy of Aquitaine, which Edward III viewed as a direct challenge to his authority and rights. In response, Edward declared himself King of France, laying claim to the French throne and asserting his position as a legitimate ruler. The formal act of war was set into motion when Edward III began to mobilize forces, leading to a series of battles, skirmishes, and political maneuvers that would define the Hundred Years' War.

Conclusion
In summary, the origins of the Hundred Years' War were deeply rooted in a combination of dynastic disputes, territorial ambitions, and economic interests. The conflicting claims to the French throne by Edward III and Philip VI, along with the desire to control lucrative territories and trade routes, created an environment ripe for war. This conflict would not only reshape the political landscape of both England and France but also set the stage for evolving national identities and the emergence of new military strategies in medieval Europe. The repercussions of these origins would resonate throughout the war, influencing the strategies, alliances, and outcomes that followed in the decades of conflict that ensued.

The Early Phase: Edwardian War
The Edwardian War, a significant segment of the Hundred Years' War, primarily unfolded during the early to mid-14th century and represented the initial phase of the protracted conflict between England and France. This period was characterized by notable battles, political maneuvers, and the emergence of new military strategies that would redefine warfare in the medieval period. Two of the most critical battles during this phase were the Battle of Crécy in 1346 and the Battle of Poitiers in 1356, both of which showcased the effectiveness of English longbowmen and the tactical innovations employed by King Edward III of England.

The Battle of Crécy (1346)
The Battle of Crécy, fought on August 26, 1346, marked a pivotal moment in the Edwardian War. Edward III, seeking to assert English claims to the French crown, launched an invasion of France. The English army, numbering approximately 10,000 men, faced a much larger French force of around 30,000 to 40,000 soldiers, which included heavily armored knights and foot soldiers.

The English forces established a strong defensive position along a ridge near the village of Crécy. Utilizing the longbow, a weapon that could shoot arrows at great distances with lethal accuracy, the English archers played a decisive role in the battle. The French, under the command of King Philip VI, launched a series of disorganized assaults against the English lines, which were met with devastating volleys of arrows. The longbowmen's ability to shoot at a rapid rate and with remarkable precision allowed them to inflict significant casualties on the French knights, who struggled to advance due to the muddy terrain and the relentless barrage of arrows.

As the battle unfolded, the morale of the French troops began to falter. The English forces, well-coordinated and resolute, capitalized on this confusion. The battle ultimately ended in a resounding victory for the English, marking a significant blow to French military prestige and establishing the longbow as a key component of English military strategy.

The Battle of Poitiers (1356)

The Battle of Poitiers, occurring on September 19, 1356, further solidified England's military dominance during the Edwardian War. The English army, led by the Black Prince, Edward, the son of Edward III, was significantly outnumbered, with roughly 8,000 troops facing an estimated 20,000 French soldiers commanded by King John II.

The Black Prince, drawing lessons from the tactics employed at Crécy, positioned his forces strategically in a defensive formation. The English troops, primarily composed of longbowmen and dismounted knights, waited for the French to engage. The French, confident in their numerical superiority, charged the English lines in a frontal assault.

As the battle commenced, the English archers unleashed a torrent of arrows, disrupting the French cavalry charge and causing chaos in their ranks. The narrow terrain further hampered the French advance, as their heavily armored knights became entangled and vulnerable. In a decisive maneuver, the Black Prince led a counterattack that exploited the disarray within the French forces, ultimately leading to a catastrophic defeat for the French.

The aftermath of the Battle of Poitiers was profound. King John II was captured and taken prisoner, a humiliation for France that would heavily influence the political landscape of the time. The English victory at Poitiers, coupled with the earlier triumph at Crécy, established Edward III as a formidable military leader and set the stage for further English advances into French territory.

Conclusion

The Early Phase of the Edwardian War, epitomized by the battles of Crécy and Poitiers, was marked by strategic innovation, particularly with the effective use of the longbow. These battles not only showcased the tactical prowess of the English but also illustrated the shifting dynamics of medieval warfare, where traditional notions of chivalric combat began to be challenged. The outcomes of these key battles had lasting repercussions for both England and France, influencing military tactics, national pride, and the course of the Hundred Years' War.

The Role of Joan of Arc

Joan of Arc, a peasant girl born around 1412 in Domrémy, France, emerged as one of the most iconic figures in history, particularly during the tumultuous period of the Hundred Years' War (1337-1453) between England and France. Her journey from obscurity to becoming a national heroine encapsulates themes of faith, nationalism, and resistance, as she played a pivotal role in revitalizing French morale and leadership during a time of despair.

Joan's early life was marked by the socio-political turmoil of the Hundred Years' War, which saw England and France embroiled in a struggle for territorial dominance. By the early 15th century, the situation for the French was dire. The English had secured significant territories, including the vital city of Paris, and the French crown was mired in internal discord, with rival factions weakening its power. It was in this context of desperation and loss that Joan claimed to have received divine visions instructing her to support Charles VII, the Dauphin of France, and to help him reclaim his throne from English control.

In 1429, Joan approached Charles VII and, despite initial skepticism, gained his trust through her unwavering conviction and fervent belief in her divine mission. She argued that she could lead an army to lift the siege of Orléans, a crucial stronghold. With the Dauphin's reluctant approval, she donned armor and took command of a French contingent. Her presence at Orléans in April 1429 marked a turning point; she inspired troops and rallied the beleaguered defenders, culminating in a decisive French victory on May 8, 1429. This triumph not only lifted the siege but also reinvigorated French hopes and morale, inspiring a sense of unity against the English forces.

Joan's influence extended beyond mere military strategy. She embodied the spirit of resistance and national identity at a time when France was fractured and disheartened. Her claims of divine guidance resonated deeply with the populace, bridging the gap between the common people and the nobility. Joan's leadership and her compelling narrative of faith and patriotism galvanized support for Charles VII, who was subsequently crowned king in Reims on July 17, 1429. This moment was significant as it symbolized not just the restoration of the monarchy but also the resurgence of French sovereignty.

However, Joan's fortunes would change dramatically. In May 1430, during a military campaign in Compiègne, she was captured by Burgundian forces, allies of the English. Joan was subsequently handed over to the English and put on trial for charges ranging from heresy to witchcraft. Her trial was politically motivated, aimed at discrediting her and, by extension, the legitimacy of Charles VII's reign. Despite the hostile environment, Joan remained steadfast, asserting her innocence and her divine mission.

On May 30, 1431, she was burned at the stake in Rouen, but her legacy only grew in the aftermath of her martyrdom. Joan of Arc became a symbol of French resistance and nationalism, her story inspiring generations. She was canonized as a saint by the Catholic Church in 1920, solidifying her status as a figure of faith and courage. Today, Joan of Arc is celebrated not only as a national heroine of France but also as a universal symbol of resistance against oppression and the fight for justice. Her life and legacy remain a testament to the profound impact one individual can have on the course of history, embodying the enduring spirit of resilience in the face of overwhelming odds.

The Lancastrian Phase and the End of the Hundred Years' War

The Lancastrian phase of the Hundred Years' War represents a significant turning point in the protracted conflict between England and France, marked by a gradual decline of English power on the continent. Beginning in the mid-15th century, this phase was characterized by political instability, military setbacks, and shifting alliances that ultimately culminated in the Treaty of Picquigny in 1475, signaling a temporary cessation of hostilities.

Decline of English Power in France

As the war progressed into the Lancastrian phase, the tide began to shift against the English. The early successes of English forces, fueled by the longbow and notable victories at battles like Crécy (1346) and Poitiers (1356), began to wane due to several factors. The most significant was the resurgence of French national identity and military effectiveness, particularly under the leadership of figures such as Charles VII, who ascended to the throne in 1422. His reign marked a departure from the earlier, disorganized French response to the English invasion.

The turning point came with the involvement of Joan of Arc, who emerged as a symbol of French resistance. Her leadership during the Siege of Orléans in 1429 galvanized French troops and shifted public morale. Joan's influence culminated in the coronation of Charles VII at Reims, which solidified his legitimacy and rallied French forces to reclaim their territories. The English, unable to match the revitalized French spirit and strategic innovations, began to suffer significant territorial losses.

Following Joan's capture and execution in 1431, the English faced a lack of unified strategy and leadership. The disparate factions within the English court, primarily the Lancastrians and Yorkists, led to internal discord that further weakened their military position. By the late 1440s, the English had lost substantial territories, including Normandy, which was formally ceded back to France under the Treaty of Picquigny.

The Treaty of Picquigny

The Treaty of Picquigny, signed in 1475, marked the end of active hostilities between England and France. This agreement was significant for several reasons. Firstly, it was a pragmatic acknowledgment of the shifting balance of power, as the English monarchy recognized the futility of continued military campaigns in France. The treaty provided for a substantial payment to the English crown from Charles VII, which served to temporarily stabilize relations between the two nations and allowed Edward IV of England to focus on domestic issues and rivalries at home.

Interestingly, the treaty also highlighted the transition from outright military conquest to diplomatic engagement. Although the English retained some territorial claims, the treaty effectively ended their aspirations to reclaim lost lands in France. The financial terms of the agreement allowed England to secure much-needed funds while simultaneously curbing further military expenditures that had drained the royal treasury.

Conclusion

The Lancastrian phase of the Hundred Years' War reflected the decline of English power in France and set the stage for the eventual cessation of hostilities through diplomatic means. The Treaty of Picquigny marked a significant moment in the evolution of international relations in Europe, illustrating how military conflict could yield to negotiations and financial agreements. As both nations moved forward, the legacies of the war would shape their futures, influencing the political landscape of Europe and paving the way for the rise of centralized nation-states in the following centuries. The end of the Hundred Years' War not only brought peace but also restored national pride in France, while England grappled with its internal strife, ultimately leading to the Wars of the Roses.

The Impact on France and England

The Hundred Years' War (1337-1453) was a protracted series of conflicts between the Kingdom of England and the Kingdom of France, characterized by territorial disputes, claims to the French throne, and the broader struggle for dominance in medieval Europe. The war had profound and lasting impacts on both nations, shaping their political landscapes, national identities, and social structures.

Political Transformation

For England, the war marked a pivotal period in its political evolution. The conflict fostered a sense of national identity, particularly as battles like Crécy and Agincourt became symbols of English valor and resilience. The English monarchy, under the leadership of kings such as Edward III and Henry V, leveraged military successes to solidify their power. However, the war also precipitated significant political strife, including the rise of the English Parliament. As the monarchy sought funds to sustain military campaigns, it increasingly relied on Parliament for financial support. This shift laid the groundwork for the development of a more participatory political system and set the stage for the eventual emergence of constitutional monarchy in England.

In contrast, France underwent a tumultuous political transformation. The devastation wrought by the war led to fragmentation and internal strife, particularly in the early phases. The French monarchy struggled to maintain authority over its territories, leading to a period of civil unrest and the rise of local powers. However, the eventual emergence of strong leadership figures, such as Joan of Arc, helped to galvanize French forces and restore national pride. By the war's conclusion, the French monarchy had consolidated power, paving the way for a more centralized state. The war catalyzed the transition from feudal allegiances to a more unified national identity, contributing to the emergence of the modern French state.

Economic Consequences

The economic ramifications of the Hundred Years' War were significant for both nations. In England, the war initially strained the economy due to the costs of military campaigns. However, the eventual victories, particularly in the early phases of the war, allowed England to expand its trade networks and territorial holdings, especially in France. The capture of key regions contributed to the growth of commerce and the development of a merchant class, which would play a crucial role in the economic transformation of England leading into the Renaissance.

Conversely, France faced severe economic hardship as a result of the war. The conflict devastated vast agricultural regions, particularly in the north, leading to food shortages and widespread suffering. The destruction of towns and infrastructure caused long-term economic challenges that would take decades to rectify. Nonetheless, the post-war period saw efforts to rebuild and recover, leading to the establishment of stronger economic policies and practices that would support the future growth of France.

Cultural and Social Shifts

Culturally, the Hundred Years' War influenced national consciousness in both nations. In England, the war fostered a burgeoning sense of nationalism, which was reflected in literature and art, notably through works like Shakespeare's "Henry V," which romanticized English heroism. The war also paved the way for the rise of English as a national language, diminishing the dominance of French in England.

In France, the war spurred a renaissance of national pride and identity, particularly through the mythos of Joan of Arc, who became a symbol of resistance and unity. Her legacy would inspire future generations and contribute to the romanticization of French nationalism.

Conclusion

In summary, the Hundred Years' War profoundly shaped the future of both France and England, influencing their political structures, economic conditions, and cultural identities. The war not only redefined the relationships between monarchy and subjects in both countries but also laid the groundwork for the emergence of nation-states that would dominate Europe in the centuries to follow. Through the trials of war, both nations found new identities that would guide their trajectories in the tumultuous landscape of European history.

Chapter 6

The Thirty Years' War

The Religious and Political Causes of the Thirty Years' War

The Thirty Years' War (1618–1648) stands as one of the most devastating conflicts in European history, marked by a complex interplay of religious and political factors that ignited widespread violence across Central Europe. Understanding the origins of this multifaceted war requires an examination of the socio-political landscape and the intense religious rivalries that characterized the period.

The Protestant Reformation

The roots of the Thirty Years' War can be traced back to the Protestant Reformation, which began in 1517 when Martin Luther nailed his Ninety-Five Theses to the church door in Wittenberg. Luther's challenge to the Catholic Church sparked a wave of religious reform that led to the establishment of various Protestant denominations. By the early 17th century, the Holy Roman Empire was a patchwork of Protestant and Catholic states, each vying for power and influence. The Peace of Augsburg in 1555 attempted to bring stability by allowing rulers to choose the religion of their own territories, yet it failed to address the underlying tensions, particularly as Calvinism emerged as a potent force alongside Lutheranism and Catholicism.

The Habsburgs and Central Authority

The political dimension of the conflict was heavily influenced by the Habsburg dynasty, which ruled both the Holy Roman Empire and a vast array of territories across Europe. The Habsburgs were staunch defenders of Catholicism, and their attempts to consolidate power often came at the expense of Protestant interests. As they sought to reassert Catholic dominance, tensions escalated, particularly in regions like Bohemia, where Protestant nobles felt increasingly threatened by Habsburg policies. The Defenestration of Prague in 1618, when Protestant nobles threw two Habsburg officials out of a window, symbolized the breakdown of negotiations and the onset of armed conflict.

The Role of External Powers

The Thirty Years' War was not merely a domestic struggle; it quickly drew in external powers exacerbating the religious and political conflicts. France, a Catholic nation, allied with Protestant states to counter Habsburg hegemony, illustrating the war's complex web of alliances. Spain, also a Habsburg power, sought to support its dynastic relatives in Austria and maintain Catholic supremacy across Europe. On the other hand, Sweden entered the war to bolster Protestant forces, while also pursuing its imperial ambitions, demonstrating how religious motivations could intertwine with national interests.

The Impact of Religion on Political Alliances
Religion played a pivotal role in shaping political alliances and enmities during the conflict. Protestant states banded together not only for self-preservation but also out of a shared ideological commitment to resist Catholic oppression. Conversely, Catholic states rallied to defend their faith and authority against a perceived Protestant threat. This intertwining of faith and politics made diplomacy difficult, as issues of allegiance often transcended mere territorial ambitions, creating a volatile environment where war became inevitable.

Conclusion
Ultimately, the Thirty Years' War was the culmination of decades of religious strife and political maneuvering within the Holy Roman Empire and beyond. The initial conflict, rooted in the tensions between Protestant and Catholic factions, quickly expanded into a broader struggle for political dominance in Europe. The war would devastate Central Europe, leading to significant shifts in power dynamics and leaving a lasting legacy on the continent's political and religious landscape. The Treaty of Westphalia, which concluded the war in 1648, not only marked the end of the conflict but also established principles of state sovereignty and religious tolerance that would shape the future of Europe. Thus, the Thirty Years' War serves as a poignant reminder of how deeply intertwined religious convictions and political ambitions can lead to widespread devastation.

Major Campaigns and Battles of the Thirty Years' War
The Thirty Years' War (1618-1648) stands as one of the most destructive conflicts of European history, marked by a series of pivotal campaigns and battles that shaped its many phases. This war was not only a struggle for territory and power but also for religious supremacy, primarily between Protestant and Catholic states within the fragmented Holy Roman Empire and beyond. The war's complexity is reflected in its numerous phases, each characterized by distinct military strategies, alliances, and key battles that would alter the course of European history.

The Bohemian Phase (1618-1625)
The war's origins can be traced to the Bohemian phase, which began with the Defenestration of Prague in 1618. This act of rebellion by Protestant nobles against the Catholic Habsburg king led to the Battle of White Mountain in 1620, a decisive confrontation that ended in a crushing defeat for the Bohemians. This battle set the tone for the early phase of the war, as the Habsburgs sought to re-establish Catholic control over the region. The defeat not only solidified Habsburg

dominance but also served as a warning to other Protestant states about the emerging threat from Catholic powers.

The Danish Phase (1625-1629)
The war escalated with the Danish phase, marked by the intervention of King Christian IV of Denmark. His arrival was motivated by a desire to support the Protestant cause and curb Habsburg influence. The key battle during this period was the Battle of Lutter in 1626, where the forces of Wallenstein achieved a significant victory over the Danes. The defeat of Danish forces led to the Edict of Restitution in 1629, which sought to restore Catholic properties lost since 1552, further inflaming tensions between Protestant and Catholic states.

The Swedish Phase (1630-1635)
The entry of Sweden under King Gustavus Adolphus marked a turning point in the Thirty Years' War. His innovative tactics and the use of mobile artillery revolutionized battlefield strategies. The Battle of Breitenfeld in 1631 was a landmark victory for the Swedish army, demonstrating their military prowess and shifting the balance of power. Gustavus Adolphus' subsequent campaigns, including the Battle of Lützen in 1632, showcased his leadership but ultimately led to his death. His passing created a vacuum in Swedish leadership, and the war continued with fluctuating fortunes for both sides.

The French Phase (1635-1648)
France's entry into the war in 1635, under Cardinal Richelieu, transformed the conflict from a primarily religious war to a political one. The French aimed to weaken Habsburg power and assert their dominance in European affairs. Notable battles during this phase included the Battle of Rocroi in 1643, where the French defeated the Spanish and marked the decline of Spanish military power in Europe. The final years of the war were characterized by a series of sieges and skirmishes, with the Treaty of Westphalia in 1648 ultimately concluding the conflict.

The Legacy of Battles
The Thirty Years' War was not merely a series of military engagements; it was a profound transformation of Europe. Major battles like White Mountain, Lutter, Breitenfeld, and Rocroi exemplified the shifting alliances and military strategies that defined the period. The war devastated large parts of Central Europe, leading to significant demographic, social, and political changes. By its conclusion, the Peace of Westphalia not only recognized the sovereignty of various states but also marked the rise of state power over religious authority, setting a precedent for the modern international system.

In summary, the major campaigns and battles of the Thirty Years' War reflect a tumultuous period of conflict that reshaped Europe's political landscape. The war's legacy is evident in its lasting impact on diplomacy, state sovereignty, and the balance of power that continues to resonate in contemporary international relations.

The Role of Foreign Powers in the Thirty Years' War

The Thirty Years' War, fought from 1618 to 1648, was one of the most devastating conflicts in European history, altering the political landscape of the continent and setting the stage for modern statehood. While the war began primarily as a religious conflict between Protestant and Catholic states within the Holy Roman Empire, it swiftly escalated into a broader struggle involving several foreign powers, each with its own interests and agendas. Key players included France, Spain, Sweden, and the Holy Roman Empire itself, whose interventions significantly influenced the war's outcome and its lasting repercussions.

France: The Catalyst of Protestant Support

France, although predominantly Catholic, emerged as a crucial player in the Thirty Years' War largely due to its geopolitical ambitions. The French monarchy, under Cardinal Richelieu, aimed to weaken the Habsburgs, who ruled both Spain and the Holy Roman Empire. Richelieu recognized that a strong Protestant presence within the Empire could counterbalance Habsburg power, and thus, he provided substantial support to Protestant factions. This included financial aid, military supplies, and diplomatic backing, effectively transforming France into a defender of Protestant interests despite its Catholic identity.

The French involvement became overt in the later stages of the war, particularly after the Swedish phase, culminating in direct military engagements against Habsburg forces. The entry of France into the war in 1635 was pivotal; it shifted the balance of power and provided the Protestant cause with much-needed reinforcement. France's involvement not only prolonged the war but also ensured that the Habsburgs would not achieve a decisive victory, ultimately leading to the Treaty of Westphalia in 1648, which favored French interests.

Spain: The Struggle for Habsburg Supremacy

Spain, under the rule of Philip IV, was another major Habsburg power involved in the Thirty Years' War. Initially, Spain sought to maintain its hegemony in Europe and support Catholic forces within the Empire. Spanish troops were dispatched to reinforce the Catholic League and combat the increasing influence of Protestant states. However, Spain's military interventions were hampered by its own overextension and the ongoing conflict with the Dutch during the Eighty Years' War.

Spanish involvement also showcased the limitations of traditional military strategies against a more mobile and adept enemy, particularly the Swedish forces led by King Gustavus Adolphus. As the war progressed, Spain faced significant challenges, including financial strain and domestic unrest, which ultimately weakened its position. By the end of the war, Spain's inability to secure a decisive victory against the Protestant states and its growing economic difficulties marked a decline in its global influence.

Sweden: The Protestant Champion
Sweden's role in the Thirty Years' War was critical, particularly through the leadership of King Gustavus Adolphus, who emerged as a champion of the Protestant cause. Motivated by both religious conviction and territorial ambitions, Sweden entered the war in 1630. Gustavus Adolphus implemented innovative military strategies, such as mobile artillery and combined arms tactics, which revolutionized warfare during this period.

The Swedish victories at battles like Breitenfeld in 1631 exemplified their military prowess and significantly bolstered the Protestant cause. However, the death of Gustavus Adolphus at the Battle of Lützen in 1632 created a leadership vacuum, leading to a more fragmented Swedish campaign. Despite this, Swedish forces continued to play an essential role in the conflict, and their eventual withdrawal did not diminish the impact they had on the war's trajectory.

The Holy Roman Empire: Internal Struggles and Fragmentation
The Holy Roman Empire, represented by the Habsburgs, faced immense challenges during the Thirty Years' War. The internal religious divisions, combined with the external pressures from foreign powers, led to a fragmentation of imperial authority. The Habsburgs' attempts to centralize control were met with fierce resistance from both Protestant princes and foreign adversaries.

As the war progressed, the Empire became increasingly dependent on foreign troops and alliances, which weakened its sovereignty. The Peace of Westphalia not only marked the end of the Thirty Years' War but also enshrined the principle of state sovereignty in Europe, fundamentally altering the balance of power and diminishing the Habsburgs' influence.

Conclusion
The involvement of foreign powers in the Thirty Years' War was crucial in shaping the conflict's outcome. France, Spain, Sweden, and the Holy Roman Empire each played distinct roles, driven by a complex mix of religious and political motivations. Their interactions and conflicts not only determined the war's dynamics but also laid the groundwork for the modern European state system, highlighting the intricate web of alliances and rivalries that characterized the era. The

war's resolution through the Peace of Westphalia fundamentally changed the political landscape of Europe, establishing a new order that emphasized state sovereignty and the balance of power—principles that continue to influence international relations today.

The Peace of Westphalia

The Peace of Westphalia, concluded in 1648, marked a pivotal moment in European history, ending the Thirty Years' War and the Eighty Years' War between Spain and the Dutch Republic. The treaties, signed in the cities of Münster and Osnabrück, not only brought an end to decades of brutal conflict but also laid the groundwork for modern statehood and international relations in Europe.

The Thirty Years' War, which began in 1618, was a complex struggle driven by a mix of religious, political, and territorial disputes. The conflict had devastated much of Central Europe, resulting in immense loss of life and widespread destruction. As the war dragged on, it became clear that a resolution was necessary to restore stability to the region. The negotiations for peace began in 1644 and involved multiple European powers, including France, Sweden, the Holy Roman Empire, and the Dutch Republic.

The treaties of Westphalia were groundbreaking in several ways. Firstly, they established the principle of state sovereignty, recognizing the authority of individual states over their territories and populations. This was a significant shift from the feudal and dynastic systems that had dominated Europe, where power was often fragmented and contested by local lords and monarchs. The Peace of Westphalia asserted that each state had the right to govern itself without outside interference, laying the foundation for the modern nation-state system.

Secondly, the treaties marked a turning point in the religious landscape of Europe. The Peace of Westphalia reaffirmed the principle of cuius regio, eius religio, which allowed rulers to determine the religion of their own states, leading to a degree of religious tolerance that had previously been absent. This principle helped to mitigate the sectarian violence that had characterized the Thirty Years' War, providing a framework for coexistence among various Christian denominations, particularly between Catholics and Protestants.

Additionally, the treaties resulted in significant territorial changes. The Holy Roman Empire lost considerable influence, and the independence of the Dutch Republic was formally recognized. Sweden emerged as a major power in Northern Europe, gaining territory and a stronger position in the Baltic region. France, too, expanded its territory, acquiring lands that would enhance its status as a dominant European power.

The impact of the Peace of Westphalia extended well beyond the immediate cessation of hostilities. It marked the beginning of a new era in international relations characterized by diplomacy and multilateral negotiations. The principles established in Westphalia influenced the development of international law and the conduct of diplomacy, fostering an environment where states could engage in dialogue rather than resorting to war.

Furthermore, the treaties set a precedent for future peace negotiations and international agreements. The concept of a balance of power began to take shape, where no single nation could dominate Europe without opposition, leading to a more stable geopolitical landscape. This balance of power would shape European politics for centuries to come, influencing alliances and conflicts through the Enlightenment, the Napoleonic Wars, and beyond.

In conclusion, the Peace of Westphalia was a watershed moment that ended a devastating conflict and fundamentally transformed European politics. By establishing the principles of state sovereignty and religious tolerance, it laid the groundwork for the modern state system and reshaped the dynamics of international relations. The legacy of Westphalia continues to resonate in contemporary discussions on sovereignty, diplomacy, and the pursuit of peace in a world still grappling with the complexities of war and conflict.

The Long-Term Consequences of the Thirty Years' War

The Thirty Years' War (1618-1648) stands as one of the most destructive conflicts in European history, resulting in catastrophic loss of life, widespread devastation, and profound political changes. The war, which began as a struggle between Catholic and Protestant states, evolved into a broader power struggle involving many of Europe's major powers. Its long-term consequences not only reshaped Central Europe but also laid critical foundations for the modern state system.

Devastation of Central Europe

The Thirty Years' War left Central Europe in ruins. The conflict ravaged the German territories, with estimates suggesting that up to 8 million people perished as a result of warfare, famine, and disease. Entire regions were depopulated; towns and villages were destroyed, and agricultural production plummeted. The economic collapse that followed severely hindered recovery efforts, as infrastructure was obliterated and trade routes disrupted.

The psychological impact on the survivors was equally profound. The war instilled a deep-seated mistrust among communities, creating a climate of fear and instability. The social fabric of many regions was irrevocably altered, as families were decimated and traditional hierarchies disrupted. The devastation of the Thirty Years' War served as a grim reminder of the catastrophic potential of religious and political strife, influencing subsequent generations' attitudes toward warfare and diplomacy.

The Peace of Westphalia: Birth of Modern Statehood

The conclusion of the Thirty Years' War was marked by the Peace of Westphalia in 1648, a series of treaties that fundamentally altered the political landscape of Europe. The agreements recognized the sovereignty of states and established the principle of non-interference in the internal affairs of other countries. This shift was pivotal in moving away from the feudal allegiances that characterized medieval Europe toward the modern concept of the nation-state.

The Peace of Westphalia effectively ended the dominance of the Catholic Church in political matters, allowing Protestant and Catholic states to coexist under their respective governance. This recognition of religious plurality laid the groundwork for secular governance and the eventual separation of church and state in many European countries. Moreover, the treaties delineated borders and recognized the sovereignty of various principalities, a notion that would become central to international relations in the centuries to come.

Shaping International Relations and Diplomacy

The war and its aftermath also fostered a new understanding of diplomacy. The multilateral negotiations that characterized the Peace of Westphalia introduced the concept of collective security and the importance of dialogue among states. The principles established during these negotiations would influence future diplomatic practices, leading to the development of international laws and organizations aimed at maintaining peace and security.

In the wake of the Thirty Years' War, the balance of power became a guiding principle of European politics. The recognition that no single state should dominate the continent led to a system of alliances and counterbalancing powers, a framework that would persist into the modern era. This balance of power theory would later influence the formation of alliances in both World Wars and shape contemporary international relations.

Conclusion

The long-term consequences of the Thirty Years' War were profound and far-reaching. The devastation of Central Europe served as a cautionary tale about the destructive potential of unchecked conflict, while the Peace of Westphalia laid the groundwork for the modern state system, emphasizing sovereignty, diplomacy, and the principles of international law. As Europe emerged from the ashes of war, the lessons learned would resonate through history, underscoring the complex interplay between warfare and the evolution of statehood and international relations. In this way, the Thirty Years' War not only reshaped the map of Europe but also contributed significantly to the frameworks that govern global interactions to this day.

Chapter 7

The Napoleonic Wars

The Rise of Napoleon Bonaparte

Napoleon Bonaparte's rise to prominence is a fascinating narrative that unfolds against the backdrop of the tumultuous events of the late 18th century, particularly the French Revolution. Born on August 15, 1769, in Corsica, a French territory, Napoleon was a member of the minor nobility. His early education in mainland France, particularly at the military academy in Brienne-le-Château and later at the École Militaire in Paris, laid the groundwork for his military career. He graduated as a second lieutenant in artillery, and his early military experiences during the French Revolutionary Wars would prove pivotal in shaping his future.

The French Revolution, which began in 1789, created a power vacuum and a chaotic political landscape in France. The revolutionary ideals of liberty, equality, and fraternity resonated deeply with Napoleon, yet he was also a pragmatist who recognized the instability and threats facing France. His opportunity to rise came during the Revolutionary Wars, particularly with the outbreak of conflict involving Austria and Prussia. In 1793, he distinguished himself in the siege of Toulon, where he played a critical role in recapturing the city from royalist forces. This victory not only showcased his military acumen but also caught the attention of influential leaders in the revolutionary government, leading to his promotion to brigadier general.

Napoleon's rapid ascent continued in the Italian campaigns of 1796-1797, where he commanded the French Army of Italy. His innovative tactics, such as the use of rapid maneuvering and surprise attacks, led to a series of stunning victories against the Austrians and their allies. The most notable of these was the battle of Marengo in 1800, where underestimating Napoleon's strategic prowess resulted in a decisive French victory. His success in Italy not only expanded French territory but also solidified his reputation as a military genius. With a series of treaties, Napoleon established French dominance in northern Italy, which effectively ended the war with Austria and earned him immense popularity in France.

The political landscape in France was precarious, marked by instability and the rise of various factions. Recognizing the need for strong leadership amidst the chaos, Napoleon returned to Paris in 1799, where he participated in the coup of 18 Brumaire. This coup d'état overthrew the Directory, the existing government, and established the Consulate, with Napoleon as one of the three consuls. However, he quickly maneuvered to consolidate power, eventually becoming the First Consul, which allowed him to wield autocratic control over France.

As First Consul, Napoleon implemented a series of reforms aimed at stabilizing the country and securing his rule. He reorganized the administrative structure, established the Napoleonic Code, and initiated educational reforms that laid the foundation for a centralized state. His domestic policies garnered widespread support and further solidified his grip on power. In 1804, he crowned himself Emperor of the French, marking the culmination of his meteoric rise and the establishment of a new monarchy that would dominate Europe.

Napoleon's ascent was characterized by a unique blend of military brilliance, political acumen, and an ability to connect with the aspirations of the French people. His rise from a relatively obscure noble to the Emperor of the French exemplified the transformative power of the Revolutionary period and set the stage for his ambitious campaigns across Europe, which would ultimately reshape the continent and leave an indelible mark on history.

The War of the Third Coalition

The War of the Third Coalition (1805-1806) marked a pivotal moment in European history, characterized by a series of significant conflicts that ultimately established Napoleon Bonaparte as one of the foremost military leaders of his time. This phase of the Napoleonic Wars was defined by the coalition of several European powers, including Great Britain, Austria, Russia, and Sweden, against France, which had been rapidly expanding under Napoleon's rule.

One of the most critical battles of the War of the Third Coalition was the Battle of Austerlitz, fought on December 2, 1805. Often referred to as the "Battle of the Three Emperors," Austerlitz pitted Napoleon's forces against the combined armies of Tsar Alexander I of Russia and Holy Roman Emperor Francis II of Austria. The battle took place near the town of Austerlitz in modern-day Czech Republic.

Napoleon, demonstrating his exceptional strategic acumen, lured the Allies into a false sense of security by appearing to weaken his right flank. As the Allies attacked this perceived vulnerability, Napoleon executed a masterful counter-offensive. His forces, numbering around 73,000, were well-coordinated and effectively used the terrain to their advantage. The French army's decisive maneuvers led to a resounding victory, resulting in approximately 36,000 casualties for the Allies compared to around 9,000 for the French. This victory solidified Napoleon's reputation and effectively dismantled the Third Coalition, forcing Austria to sign the Treaty of Pressburg, which ceded significant territories to France and its allies.

In contrast, the naval engagement at the Battle of Trafalgar, fought on October 21, 1805, represented a critical moment for British maritime supremacy. The British Royal Navy, under Admiral Horatio Nelson, faced the combined fleets of France and Spain near the Strait of Gibraltar. The stakes were high, as control of the seas was essential for the British to continue their fight against Napoleon's ambitions.

Admiral Nelson devised an unorthodox strategy by dividing his fleet into two columns to break the enemy line, a tactic that would enable his ships to engage the enemy at close quarters. The British fleet, numbering 27 ships, was outnumbered but possessed superior tactics and seamanship. The battle culminated in a decisive British victory, with the loss of 22 ships from the Franco-Spanish fleet compared to none from the British.

The significance of Trafalgar extended beyond the immediate military consequences. It effectively ended Napoleon's plans for invading Britain and confirmed British naval dominance for over a century. Tragically, Admiral Nelson was mortally wounded during the battle, but his legacy as a national hero was cemented, and his tactics continued to influence naval warfare.

In conclusion, the War of the Third Coalition showcased the contrasting theaters of land and sea warfare during this tumultuous period in European history. The victories at Austerlitz and Trafalgar not only exemplified the strategic brilliance of Napoleon and Nelson but also shaped the geopolitical landscape of Europe. While Napoleon's triumph at Austerlitz reinforced his control over continental Europe, the British victory at Trafalgar secured their maritime supremacy, setting the stage for a protracted conflict that would shape the future of nations and the very essence of warfare. The legacies of these battles continue to resonate in military studies and the broader narrative of European history.

The Peninsular War and the Invasion of Russia

The Napoleonic Wars marked a pivotal era in military history, characterized by rapid movement, grand strategies, and the profound impact of leadership. Among the most significant turning points in Napoleon Bonaparte's campaigns were the Peninsular War (1808-1814) and the ill-fated invasion of Russia in 1812. Both conflicts not only showcased the strengths and weaknesses of Napoleon's military genius but also contributed to the eventual decline of his empire.

The Peninsular War: A Quagmire

The Peninsular War began with Napoleon's ambition to consolidate control over Spain and Portugal. In 1808, he installed his brother Joseph Bonaparte as king of Spain, inciting widespread resistance among the Spanish population. This conflict quickly transformed into a protracted guerrilla war, as Spanish partisans fought against French forces using unconventional tactics that exploited their knowledge of local terrain. The British, under the leadership of General Arthur Wellesley, later known as the Duke of Wellington, supported the Spanish resistance with troops and supplies, complicating Napoleon's efforts to maintain control.

The war became a significant drain on French resources and morale. While Napoleon was known for his rapid and decisive campaigns, the nature of the Peninsular War required a different approach. The French forces found themselves engaged in a war of attrition, facing not only the organized armies of Spain and Britain but also the relentless guerrilla warfare that sapped their strength and resolve. Key battles, such as the Battle of Salamanca in 1812, highlighted the tactical prowess of Wellington and the challenges faced by the French.

The Peninsular War also had profound political ramifications. It inspired nationalist sentiments across Europe, contributing to a growing tide of resistance against French hegemony. The conflict drained French manpower and resources, leaving Napoleon's forces stretched thin as they faced growing opposition in other parts of Europe.

The Invasion of Russia: Overreach and Catastrophe

The 1812 invasion of Russia marked a dramatic escalation in Napoleon's ambitions. Motivated by the desire to enforce the Continental System—an economic blockade against Britain—Napoleon assembled the Grande Armée, one of the largest military forces ever mobilized. The invasion initially showcased the might of French military power, with decisive victories at battles such as Smolensk. However, the campaign soon unraveled due to logistical challenges, harsh weather conditions, and scorched-earth tactics employed by the retreating Russian forces.

The pivotal moment of the invasion was the disastrous retreat from Moscow. After capturing the Russian capital, which had been largely abandoned and set ablaze, Napoleon found himself unable to sustain his army in the face of the brutal Russian winter. The retreat turned into a harrowing ordeal, with the Grande Armée suffering catastrophic losses from starvation, exposure, and Russian attacks. By the time the remnants of the army crossed back into friendly territory, they had lost approximately 500,000 men—an irrevocable blow to Napoleon's military might.

The failures in both the Peninsular War and the Russian campaign illustrated a critical turning point in Napoleon's fortunes. His overreaching ambitions, coupled with underestimating the resilience of his adversaries and the harsh realities of warfare, set the stage for his eventual downfall. The combination of sustained resistance in Spain and the catastrophic losses in Russia fractured the seemingly invincible aura surrounding Napoleon, emboldening coalitions of European powers to rise against him.

In summary, the Peninsular War and the invasion of Russia represent key turning points in Napoleon's military campaigns, revealing the vulnerabilities of an empire built on rapid conquest and centralized control. These conflicts not only drained resources and morale but also ignited nationalist movements that would challenge French dominance, ultimately leading to the unraveling of Napoleon's empire.

The Fall of Napoleon

The fall of Napoleon Bonaparte marked a pivotal turning point in European history, culminating in the Battle of Waterloo and the Congress of Vienna. Napoleon's ambitious expansion of the French Empire had begun to unravel, attributed to a combination of military overreach, strategic miscalculations, and the resurgence of coalitions against him. This section examines the decisive events that led to his downfall and the subsequent efforts to restore order in Europe.

The Battle of Waterloo

The Battle of Waterloo, fought on June 18, 1815, in present-day Belgium, was the climactic confrontation of the Napoleonic Wars. Following his escape from exile on the island of Elba, Napoleon returned to France in March 1815, rallying his supporters and reclaiming power. His return prompted an alliance of European powers, known as the Seventh Coalition, which included Britain, Prussia, the Netherlands, and other states determined to stop his resurgence.

Napoleon faced a formidable coalition army led by the Duke of Wellington and the Prussian Field Marshal Gebhard Leberecht von Blücher. The battle itself was characterized by intense fighting, marked by the strategic use of terrain and troop formations. Wellington's forces, despite being outnumbered initially, utilized defensive tactics effectively until the arrival of Blücher's Prussian army turned the tide.

As the day progressed, Napoleon's forces suffered from poor coordination and the inability to secure victory against the combined might of the allied troops. The decisive moment came with the collapse of the French right flank, leading to a chaotic retreat. The loss at Waterloo effectively ended Napoleon's rule and led to his second abdication. He was subsequently exiled to the remote island of Saint Helena in the South Atlantic, where he would spend the remainder of his life.

The Congress of Vienna

The Congress of Vienna, convened in 1814 and concluding in 1815, was a diplomatic gathering of the major powers of Europe aimed at reestablishing stability and order after the upheaval caused by the Napoleonic Wars. The primary architects of the Congress were the foreign ministers of Austria, Russia, Prussia, and Great Britain: Klemens von Metternich, Tsar Alexander I, Prince Karl von Hardenberg, and Lord Castlereagh. Their collective goal was to create a balance of power that would prevent any single nation from dominating Europe as France had under Napoleon.

Key principles of the Congress included the restoration of monarchies, redrawing of national boundaries, and the establishment of a framework for international diplomacy. The leaders sought to contain revolutionary fervor and maintain the status quo through a network of alliances and agreements, notably the Holy Alliance between Russia, Austria, and Prussia, which aimed to uphold Christian values and monarchic authority.

The decisions made at the Congress of Vienna had lasting implications for Europe. The territorial adjustments made to the map of Europe aimed to ensure a balance of power, leading to a century of relative peace in the continent, often referred to as the "Concert of Europe." However, these adjustments also sowed the seeds for future conflicts, particularly due to nationalist sentiments that arose from the arbitrary nature of borders drawn by the Congress.

Conclusion
The fall of Napoleon Bonaparte and the subsequent Congress of Vienna reshaped Europe's political landscape. The Battle of Waterloo symbolized not only the end of an era of Napoleonic dominance but also the complex interplay of military strategy and diplomacy. The Congress established a framework for international relations that sought to maintain peace, yet the echoes of revolutionary ideas and nationalist aspirations would continue to influence European politics in the decades to come. Ultimately, the legacy of these events underscores the dynamic nature of power and governance in the context of war and peace.

The Legacy of the Napoleonic Wars

The Napoleonic Wars, spanning from 1803 to 1815, left an indelible mark on Europe and the world, fundamentally reshaping political landscapes, societal structures, and military strategies. The legacy of these conflicts is multifaceted, encompassing the rise of nationalism, the transformation of warfare, and the reconfiguration of international relations.

At the heart of the legacy of the Napoleonic Wars is the rise of nationalism. As Napoleon expanded his empire across Europe, he inadvertently incited nationalistic sentiments in the very nations he sought to dominate. The imposition of French laws and reforms, such as the Napoleonic Code, often met with resistance, awakening a sense of collective identity among various peoples. For example, the liberation movements in Spain and Italy drew inspiration from the desire to resist foreign domination and assert national sovereignty. The concept of the nation-state emerged more prominently, leading to the eventual unification of Germany and Italy in the latter half of the 19th century. This wave of nationalism would continue to shape European politics and conflicts, culminating in both World Wars.

The Napoleonic Wars also revolutionized military tactics and organization. The conflicts marked a significant shift from traditional linear warfare to more dynamic forms of combat. Napoleon's use of rapid troop movements, combined arms, and decisive battles set new standards for military engagements. His emphasis on meritocracy within the military ranks led to the professionalization of armies across Europe. This transformation influenced military doctrines and strategies in subsequent conflicts, as nations sought to emulate the successes of the French army. Moreover, the extensive use of conscription during the wars highlighted the need for larger standing armies, a trend that would persist into the 20th century.

The political ramifications of the Napoleonic Wars were profound, leading to the Congress of Vienna in 1815, which aimed to restore a balance of power in Europe and prevent further large-scale conflicts. The Congress established a diplomatic framework that prioritized collective security and cooperation among the major powers, laying the groundwork for modern international relations. However, the decisions made at Vienna also set the stage for future tensions, as the suppression of nationalist movements in various regions created underlying grievances that would erupt in subsequent revolutions.

Economically, the Napoleonic Wars had lasting effects on European states. The conflicts disrupted trade routes and led to significant economic hardship in many regions. However, the subsequent industrialization that followed in the 19th century can, in part, be attributed to the need for nations to rebuild and modernize their economies post-war. The wars also spurred developments in logistics and supply chains, which would play crucial roles in future military conflicts.

The global influence of the Napoleonic Wars extended beyond Europe. In the Americas, the wars contributed to the independence movements in Latin America, as colonial powers were weakened and distracted by European conflicts. The Haitian Revolution, which was partly a response to French policies, also marked a significant moment in the struggle against colonialism and slavery. The ideas of liberty, equality, and fraternity propagated by the French Revolution found resonance in various independence movements around the globe.

In conclusion, the legacy of the Napoleonic Wars is characterized by the profound effects on national identity, military strategy, political structures, and global relations. These conflicts not only reshaped Europe but also set into motion trends and ideas that would echo through the ages, influencing the trajectory of world history in the 19th and 20th centuries. The lessons learned from the Napoleonic era continue to resonate in contemporary discussions around nationalism, warfare, and international diplomacy, reminding us of the complex interplay between conflict and societal evolution.

Chapter 8

The American Civil War

The Causes of the Civil War
The American Civil War, a watershed moment in the history of the United States, was driven by a confluence of factors, with slavery at its core. The institution of slavery had been a contentious issue since the nation's founding, creating deep divisions between the Northern and Southern states. While the North increasingly moved toward industrialization and a labor system that did not rely on enslaved people, the South remained agrarian, heavily dependent on slave labor for its economy. This fundamental economic disparity fostered contrasting social, political, and cultural ideologies that ultimately culminated in conflict.

Slavery as a Central Issue
At the heart of the Civil War was the question of slavery. The Southern economy was built on the backs of enslaved individuals, particularly in the production of cotton, which became the South's primary cash crop. As the demand for cotton surged, so too did the demand for slave labor. The North, on the other hand, increasingly viewed slavery as morally reprehensible. Abolitionist movements gained momentum in the early to mid-19th century, advocating for the emancipation of enslaved people and the end of the institution altogether. Prominent figures such as Frederick Douglass and Harriet Tubman emerged as leaders in the fight against slavery, further polarizing the nation.

Legislation regarding slavery also fueled tensions. The Missouri Compromise of 1820 and the Compromise of 1850 attempted to maintain a balance between free and slave states but ultimately sowed the seeds of discord. The introduction of the Kansas-Nebraska Act in 1854, which allowed territories to decide for themselves whether to allow slavery, led to violent confrontations known as "Bleeding Kansas." These events highlighted the inability of the nation to find a peaceful resolution to the slavery issue, deepening the rift between North and South.

States' Rights and Regional Identity
The concept of states' rights emerged as another significant factor contributing to the Civil War. Southern states championed the idea that states had the authority to govern themselves and make their own laws, particularly regarding slavery. This belief was rooted in the interpretation of the Constitution, which many Southern leaders argued protected their rights to maintain their social and economic systems.

As the federal government took steps to limit the expansion of slavery and promote federal authority, Southern states perceived these measures as threats to their autonomy. The notion that states could secede from the Union if they disagreed with federal policies gained traction, leading to a sense of regional identity that prioritized Southern interests. This growing sentiment was crystallized in the formation of the Confederacy, where states emphasized their right to self-governance over the authority of the federal government.

Cultural and Political Divisions

The cultural differences between the North and South further exacerbated tensions. The South's agrarian society, with its reliance on slavery, fostered a distinct culture that valued tradition and hierarchical social structures. In contrast, the North embraced industrialization, urbanization, and a more egalitarian ethos. These cultural disparities manifested in political disagreements, with differing views on tariffs, infrastructure development, and economic policies.

The election of Abraham Lincoln in 1860, perceived by Southern states as a direct threat to slavery, acted as a catalyst for secession. Lincoln's commitment to halting the expansion of slavery alarmed Southern leaders, prompting several states to secede and form the Confederate States of America. This decisive action ultimately led to the outbreak of war in April 1861.

In conclusion, the American Civil War was rooted in a complex interplay of factors, primarily centered on slavery and states' rights. The economic, social, and political divisions between the North and South created an environment ripe for conflict. Understanding these causes is crucial for comprehending the profound impact of the Civil War on American society and its legacy in shaping the nation's future.

Major Battles and Campaigns of the American Civil War

The American Civil War (1861-1865) was marked by numerous pivotal battles that not only shaped the course of the conflict but also had profound implications for the future of the United States. Among these, the battles of Gettysburg and Antietam stand out as crucial turning points, alongside other significant military engagements that defined the war's trajectory.

The Battle of Antietam (September 17, 1862)

Antietam, fought in Maryland, holds the grim distinction of being the bloodiest single day in American military history, with approximately 22,000 casualties. This battle emerged from Confederate General Robert E. Lee's first invasion of the North, aiming to secure a decisive victory that would bolster Southern morale and potentially sway European powers to recognize the Confederacy. The Union Army, under General George McClellan, engaged Lee's forces in a series of fierce confrontations near Antietam Creek. The battle saw intense fighting in key locations, notably at the Cornfield, the Sunken Road, and Burnside's Bridge. Although the battle ended inconclusively, with Lee retreating back to Virginia, it provided President Abraham Lincoln the political leverage needed to announce the Emancipation Proclamation, fundamentally changing the war's focus to include the abolition of slavery.

The Battle of Gettysburg (July 1-3, 1863)

Gettysburg is often considered the turning point of the Civil War. Occurring in Pennsylvania, it marked the culmination of Lee's second invasion of the North. The battle unfolded over three harrowing days, with the Union Army, commanded by General George G. Meade, positioning itself advantageously against Lee's troops. Key engagements included the fierce fighting on Cemetery Hill, Little Round Top, and Pickett's Charge, where Confederate forces made a desperate but ultimately disastrous assault on the center of the Union line on the third day. The Union's victory at Gettysburg halted Lee's advance and turned the tide in favor of the North, inflicting significant casualties on the Confederate Army, which would struggle to replenish its ranks in the subsequent years.

The Battle of Vicksburg (May 18 - July 4, 1863)

While Gettysburg was a key confrontation in the East, the Siege of Vicksburg in Mississippi was equally pivotal in the West. The Union, under General Ulysses S. Grant, aimed to capture this strategic stronghold on the Mississippi River to split the Confederacy and gain control of vital supply routes. After a grueling campaign involving multiple assaults and a prolonged siege, Vicksburg surrendered on July 4, 1863, coinciding with the Union victory at Gettysburg. This dual victory significantly boosted Northern morale and enabled the Union to control the Mississippi River, effectively isolating Texas, Louisiana, and Arkansas from the rest of the Confederacy.

The Battle of Chickamauga (September 19-20, 1863)

Chickamauga, fought in Georgia, was another major confrontation that saw the Confederate Army achieving a significant victory over Union forces commanded by General William Rosecrans. After a series of miscommunications and tactical mistakes, the Union army was forced to retreat to Chattanooga. The battle was characterized by fierce fighting and high casualties, with the Confederates under General Braxton Bragg gaining the upper hand. However, this victory was short-lived, as subsequent Union reinforcements would lead to a Union victory at Chattanooga later that year.

The Battle of Atlanta (July 22 - September 2, 1864)

The campaign for Atlanta was crucial for General William Tecumseh Sherman and the Union's strategy to disrupt the South's industrial capabilities. The fall of Atlanta not only served as a significant military victory but also had political implications, bolstering Northern support for the war effort during an election year.

These battles, among others, played a critical role in determining the outcome of the Civil War, showcasing the complexities of military strategy, leadership, and the evolving nature of warfare during this tumultuous period in American history. Each engagement contributed to the larger narrative of a nation torn apart, grappling with issues of unity, freedom, and the very identity of its citizenry.

The Role of Abraham Lincoln in the American Civil War

Abraham Lincoln, the 16th President of the United States, played a pivotal role in the American Civil War, a conflict that not only defined a nation but also tested its very principles. His leadership during this tumultuous period was characterized by a steadfast commitment to preserving the Union and abolishing slavery, two intertwined issues that defined the fabric of American society.

Leadership Style and Political Strategy

Lincoln's leadership style was marked by pragmatism, empathy, and a deep understanding of the political landscape. He faced immense challenges, including a divided nation, an unprepared military, and opposition from both Northern Democrats and radical abolitionists. His ability to navigate these complexities was crucial for maintaining support for the war effort. Lincoln famously surrounded himself with a "Team of Rivals," consisting of former political adversaries, which allowed him to incorporate diverse viewpoints and foster a collaborative environment in his administration. This strategy not only helped to unify the Republican Party but also facilitated the development of effective military strategies and political policies.

Commitment to the Union

From the outset of the war, Lincoln was resolute in his belief that the Union must be preserved at all costs. His initial focus was on restoring the Union rather than directly addressing the issue of slavery. However, as the war progressed and the moral implications of slavery became increasingly apparent, Lincoln recognized that the emancipation of enslaved people was not only a moral imperative but also a strategic necessity. He understood that abolishing slavery would weaken the Confederate war effort, which relied heavily on slave labor.

Emancipation Proclamation

Lincoln's issuance of the Emancipation Proclamation on January 1, 1863, was a landmark moment in the Civil War and American history. By declaring that all enslaved people in the Confederate states were to be freed, Lincoln transformed the war into a moral crusade against slavery. While the Proclamation did not immediately free all enslaved individuals, it fundamentally altered the character of the conflict, allowing African Americans to join the Union Army and contributing to the eventual abolition of slavery through the 13th Amendment. This bold move not only galvanized support for the Union cause but also redefined the purpose of the war, rallying anti-slavery sentiments in the North and among European nations that were considering support for the Confederacy.

Impact on Military Strategy

Lincoln's involvement in military strategy was another critical aspect of his leadership. He took an active role in the selection of generals and the planning of military campaigns, often learning from early missteps and adjusting tactics accordingly. For instance, after the Union defeat at the Battle of Bull Run, he recognized the need for more effective leadership and appointed General George B. McClellan to command the Army of the Potomac. Although McClellan's cautious approach frustrated Lincoln, it reflected the president's willingness to experiment with military strategies and take calculated risks.

Legacy and Conclusion

Lincoln's leadership during the Civil War left an indelible mark on the United States. His ability to articulate the moral and political stakes of the conflict helped to unify the North and maintain public support for the war effort, even in the face of significant setbacks. By the time of his assassination in 1865, Lincoln had not only preserved the Union but had also set the stage for a new era of civil rights and reconstruction. His vision for a united nation, free from the scourge of slavery, continues to resonate in contemporary discussions about equality and justice.

In summary, Abraham Lincoln's leadership was instrumental in shaping the outcome of the Civil War. His commitment to the Union, strategic use of executive power, and moral clarity regarding slavery fundamentally altered the trajectory of American history, establishing him as one of the nation's most revered leaders.

The Emancipation Proclamation

The Emancipation Proclamation, issued by President Abraham Lincoln on January 1, 1863, marked a pivotal turning point in the American Civil War, transforming the conflict from a battle for the preservation of the Union into a moral crusade against the institution of slavery. This executive order declared that all enslaved people in the Confederate states were to be set free, fundamentally altering the war's purpose and its implications for American society.

Historical Context and Motivations
At the onset of the Civil War in 1861, Lincoln's primary objective was to preserve the Union rather than to abolish slavery. However, as the war progressed, the realities of armed conflict and the moral weight of slavery began to shift public opinion and political strategy. The Union faced significant challenges on the battlefield, and the enlistment of Black soldiers became increasingly important for bolstering Union forces. The plight of enslaved individuals, who were often forced to work for the Confederate war effort, underscored the necessity of addressing slavery as a tactical and ethical imperative.

Lincoln's personal views on slavery evolved over time. Although he was initially cautious about emancipation due to fears of alienating border states and moderates, he recognized that freeing enslaved people would undermine the Confederacy and strengthen the Union's military capacity. The Proclamation was also a strategic move aimed at preventing foreign powers, particularly Britain and France, from intervening on behalf of the Confederacy by framing the war in moral terms.

The Proclamation Itself
The Emancipation Proclamation stated that all persons held as slaves in rebellious states "shall be then, thenceforward, and forever free." Importantly, this declaration applied only to the states in rebellion and not to the border states loyal to the Union or areas already under Union control. Consequently, while it did not immediately free a single enslaved person, it signaled a critical shift in policy and purpose.

The Proclamation also allowed for the recruitment of Black soldiers into the Union Army, which proved to be a significant advantage. By the end of the war, nearly 200,000 Black soldiers and sailors had served in the Union, contributing to the war effort and reshaping the narrative surrounding African Americans' roles in the military and society.

Impact and Legacy
The Emancipation Proclamation had profound repercussions. It galvanized the abolitionist movement and provided a moral framework for the Union's war efforts. The document inspired enslaved individuals to escape to Union lines, where they could find freedom and contribute to the war effort. It also shifted the focus of the war, aligning it with the ideals of liberty and equality enshrined in the Declaration of Independence.

The Proclamation laid the groundwork for the eventual passage of the Thirteenth Amendment in 1865, which abolished slavery throughout the United States. As the war drew to a close, the Union victory was not only a triumph for the preservation of the nation but also a monumental step toward civil rights and social justice.

In conclusion, the Emancipation Proclamation was not just a military strategy; it was a moral declaration that redefined the Civil War's objectives. It transformed the conflict into a fight not only for national unity but also for human freedom, establishing a precedent for future civil rights movements and shaping the trajectory of American history. The legacy of the Proclamation continues to resonate, reminding us of the ongoing struggle for equality and justice in a nation still grappling with the repercussions of its past.

The Reconstruction Era

The Reconstruction Era, spanning from 1865 to 1877, was a pivotal period in American history, marked by the complex challenges of reuniting a nation that had been torn apart by the Civil War. As the Union emerged victorious, it faced the daunting task of integrating millions of newly freed African Americans into society and addressing the political, economic, and social upheavals that followed the war.

One of the most pressing challenges during Reconstruction was the question of how to reintegrate the Southern states into the Union. The federal government had to determine the terms under which these states could regain their political status. The differing views on this issue among political leaders created significant tension. President Abraham Lincoln advocated for a lenient approach, proposing the Ten Percent Plan, which allowed Southern states to rejoin the Union if 10% of their voters pledged allegiance to the Union. However, Lincoln's assassination in April 1865 shifted the power dynamics, and his successor, Andrew Johnson, implemented a more lenient policy that failed to address the needs of formerly enslaved individuals.

Conversely, Congress, particularly the Radical Republicans, believed that a more stringent approach was necessary. They sought to impose stricter conditions on Southern states, including the requirement to ratify the Fourteenth Amendment, which granted citizenship to all persons born in the United States, and the Fifteenth Amendment, which aimed to secure voting rights for African American men. This conflict between presidential and congressional policies led to significant political strife, culminating in Johnson's impeachment in 1868.

The social landscape of the South was profoundly transformed during Reconstruction as the newly freed African Americans sought to exercise their rights and improve their living conditions. However, the transition was fraught with obstacles. The establishment of the Freedmen's Bureau aimed to assist former slaves in securing education, employment, and legal rights. While it achieved some successes, such as setting up schools and providing medical care, the Bureau faced immense opposition from white Southerners who were resistant to the changes brought about by emancipation.

Racial tensions escalated as white supremacist groups, most notably the Ku Klux Klan, emerged to terrorize African Americans and suppress their newfound freedoms. These groups employed violence and intimidation, aiming to restore white dominance in the South. The federal government responded with the Enforcement Acts, which aimed to protect African Americans' rights, but the effectiveness of these measures was limited, as enforcement was often inconsistent.

Economically, the South struggled to recover from the devastation of the Civil War. The old plantation system was dismantled, and a new labor system emerged, characterized by sharecropping and tenant farming. Many African Americans became sharecroppers, cultivating land they did not own in exchange for a share of the crops. This system often perpetuated cycles of poverty and debt, limiting the economic mobility of African Americans and white farmers alike.

As the Reconstruction Era progressed into the 1870s, political support for Reconstruction waned in the North. Economic concerns, the Panic of 1873, and a growing desire to move on from the issues of the Civil War led many to abandon the commitment to enforcing civil rights in the South. The Compromise of 1877, which resolved the contentious presidential election of 1876, effectively ended Reconstruction. In exchange for the presidency, Republican Rutherford B. Hayes agreed to withdraw federal troops from the South, paving the way for the return of white Democratic control and the establishment of Jim Crow laws that enforced racial segregation.

In conclusion, the Reconstruction Era was a complex and challenging time for the United States as it attempted to heal the wounds of war and redefine its national identity. The struggle for African Americans to secure their rights, the political conflicts between different factions, and the economic difficulties faced by the South collectively shaped the course of American history. The legacies of Reconstruction would resonate for generations, influencing civil rights movements and shaping the ongoing struggle for equality in the United States.

Chapter 9

World War I

The Origins of the Great War
The origins of World War I, often referred to as the Great War, are deeply rooted in a complex web of alliances, nationalistic fervor, imperial ambitions, and political tensions that had been building for decades prior to the outbreak of hostilities in 1914. The assassination of Archduke Franz Ferdinand of Austria-Hungary on June 28, 1914, served as the immediate catalyst for the war, but it was the culmination of underlying factors that set the stage for a conflict of unprecedented scale.

Alliances and Ententes
By the early 20th century, Europe was characterized by a precarious balance of power, maintained through a series of alliances designed to deter aggression and maintain peace. The most significant alliances were the Triple Alliance, comprising Germany, Austria-Hungary, and Italy, and the Triple Entente, which included France, Russia, and Great Britain. These alliances were not merely military agreements; they were also political commitments that obligated member states to support one another in times of crisis. The entanglement of these alliances meant that a conflict involving one nation could quickly draw in others, escalating regional disputes into a full-blown war.

Nationalism
Nationalism played a crucial role in the lead-up to the Great War. The late 19th and early 20th centuries were marked by a surge in national pride and an intense desire for national unification or independence. In Austria-Hungary, various ethnic groups sought autonomy, creating internal tensions that threatened the stability of the empire. At the same time, Serbia, with its Slavic population and pan-Slavic aspirations, posed a direct challenge to Austro-Hungarian authority. The desire for national recognition and the belief in the superiority of one's nation fueled hostility and competition among the great powers.

Imperial Rivalries
The competition for overseas colonies and resources intensified rivalries among European powers. The late 19th century witnessed a scramble for Africa and an expansion of empires in Asia, leading to heightened tensions, particularly between Britain, France, and Germany. The Moroccan Crises in 1905 and 1911 exemplified this imperial competition, as Germany attempted

to challenge French influence in Morocco, only to be met with a united front from Britain and France. These conflicts further entrenched animosities and fostered a sense of impending confrontation.

The Balkan Wars
The Balkan region became a flashpoint for conflict in the years leading up to World War I. The decline of the Ottoman Empire led to the rise of nationalist movements and territorial disputes among Balkan states. The Balkan Wars (1912-1913) saw Serbia, Bulgaria, Greece, and Montenegro fighting for territory, which significantly altered the balance of power in Southeastern Europe. Serbia's territorial gains, in particular, alarmed Austria-Hungary, which perceived Serbia as a growing threat to its own stability and influence in the region.

The Assassination
The assassination of Archduke Franz Ferdinand by Gavrilo Princip, a Bosnian Serb nationalist, was the spark that ignited the powder keg. Austria-Hungary, seeking to curb Serbian nationalism and assert its dominance, issued an ultimatum to Serbia with demands that were intentionally harsh. Serbia's response, though conciliatory, was deemed insufficient by Austria-Hungary, leading to the declaration of war on July 28, 1914. The rigid alliances that had formed in the preceding decades transformed this regional conflict into a world war, as Russia mobilized to support Serbia, Germany declared war on Russia, and France was drawn in against Germany.

In summary, the origins of the Great War were not simply a matter of one assassination but rather the result of a complex interplay of alliances, nationalism, imperial ambitions, and regional conflicts. This intricate tapestry of factors created a volatile environment that made war not only likely but almost inevitable, setting the stage for a conflict that would reshape the world.

Trench Warfare and Major Battles
The Western Front of World War I became infamous for its grueling trench warfare, a combat style that defined the conflict and exemplified the horrors of modern warfare. As the war progressed, both the Allied and Central Powers found themselves locked in a stalemate, leading to a protracted series of battles characterized by the extensive use of trenches as defensive fortifications. The conditions of trench warfare not only shaped military strategies but also had profound effects on the soldiers' morale and the overall outcome of the war.

The Nature of Trench Warfare
Trench warfare was born out of a necessity to protect soldiers from the lethal advancements in weaponry, including machine guns, artillery, and later, chemical weapons. The trenches extended from the North Sea to Switzerland, creating a static front line that was difficult to breach. Soldiers lived in squalid conditions, enduring mud, vermin, and the constant threat of enemy fire. The front was often divided into three main lines: the front line, support trench, and reserve trench, with communication trenches linking these positions.

The psychological toll of living in these trenches was immense. Soldiers faced not only the physical dangers of warfare but also the fear and anxiety that came from the relentless bombardment and the ever-present possibility of death. The brutal conditions of trench life, combined with the incessant nature of the fighting, contributed to a significant decline in morale.

The Battle of Verdun
One of the most significant battles on the Western Front was the Battle of Verdun, fought from February to December 1916. This battle became a symbol of French national determination and resilience. The German strategy aimed to bleed France white, inflicting heavy casualties in a battle of attrition. The French, under the leadership of General Philippe Pétain, famously declared, "They shall not pass!" in a rallying call to defend the fortress city of Verdun.

The battle was marked by relentless fighting and horrific casualties, with estimates of around 700,000 total casualties. The landscape around Verdun was transformed into a desolate wasteland, littered with the remnants of war. The sheer scale of suffering and the strategic stalemate exemplified the futility of trench warfare. Although the French ultimately held Verdun, the battle left deep scars on the national psyche and highlighted the horrors of the conflict.

The Battle of the Somme
The Battle of the Somme, launched on July 1, 1916, was one of the largest battles of World War I and exemplified the tragic cost of trench warfare. The first day of the battle remains the bloodiest in British military history, with nearly 60,000 British casualties. The objective was to relieve pressure on the French forces at Verdun and to break through German defenses.

Despite the initial hopes for a breakthrough, the battle quickly devolved into yet another stalemate. The Allies faced formidable German defenses, and the tactic of "going over the top" from the trenches often resulted in mass casualties. The battle continued until November, resulting in over one million men wounded or killed. The Somme epitomized the brutal nature of

World War I, where technological advancements in warfare outpaced strategies for effectively employing them.

Conclusion

The experiences of trench warfare on the Western Front, particularly during the Battles of Verdun and the Somme, underscored the devastating realities of World War I. The combination of brutal living conditions, staggering casualties, and the psychological impact on soldiers created a backdrop of despair and futility. These battles not only shaped military tactics but also left an indelible mark on the collective memory of nations involved, leading to a profound reflection on the nature of war and its human cost. As the war dragged on, the lessons learned from these engagements would echo throughout military history, influencing future conflicts and the approach to warfare itself.

The Role of Technology in World War I

World War I, often referred to as the Great War, marked a pivotal turning point in military history, characterized by the unprecedented integration of technology into warfare. The industrial revolution had laid the groundwork for significant advancements, but it was during this conflict that many of these innovations were put to the test on a global scale. The introduction and utilization of tanks, airplanes, and chemical weapons fundamentally transformed the nature of combat, strategies, and the overall experience of war for soldiers and civilians alike.

Tanks: Breaking the Stalemate

One of the most significant technological innovations of WWI was the introduction of the tank. Developed in response to the trench warfare that characterized the Western Front, tanks were designed to overcome the barbed wire defenses and machine gun nests that had rendered traditional infantry assaults futile. The first tanks were deployed by the British at the Battle of the Somme in 1916. Although they were initially slow and mechanically unreliable, tanks represented a new approach to warfare that combined mobility with firepower.

The psychological impact of tanks was also substantial. Their presence on the battlefield instilled fear in enemy troops while providing a morale boost to their own forces. As the war progressed, advancements in tank design led to improved speed, armor, and firepower, culminating in more effective armored assaults in the later stages of the war. By the conflict's end, tanks had begun to reshape battlefield tactics and would continue to do so in subsequent conflicts.

Airplanes: The New Frontier

The advent of aviation during WWI introduced a new dimension to warfare. Initially used for reconnaissance missions, airplanes quickly evolved to serve multiple purposes, including ground attack and aerial dogfighting. The famous dogfights between fighter pilots, such as the exploits of the Red Baron, captured public imagination and highlighted the growing importance of air superiority.

Bombers also began to play a crucial role, targeting enemy infrastructure and troop concentrations from above. The introduction of aerial technology not only changed military strategy but also allowed for the first instances of total war, where civilian targets could be attacked to disrupt the enemy's economy and morale. The strategic use of airplanes laid the foundation for the role of air power in future conflicts, emphasizing its importance in modern warfare.

Chemical Weapons: A Grim Innovation

Perhaps one of the most notorious technological developments during WWI was the introduction of chemical weapons. Chlorine gas was first used by the Germans at the Second Battle of Ypres in 1915, marking a horrific new chapter in warfare. The use of gas was intended to instill terror and cause chaos among enemy troops, and its effectiveness led to widespread adoption by both sides.

Chemical weapons posed unique challenges for soldiers, who were often unprepared for the psychological and physical effects of gas attacks. The introduction of gas masks became a necessity, highlighting the grim reality of modern warfare. Although chemical weapons were not as decisive in terms of achieving military objectives, their use raised ethical questions about the conduct of war and influenced international law regarding warfare in the years to come.

Conclusion

The technological innovations of World War I had far-reaching implications, fundamentally altering the landscape of military conflict. The introduction of tanks, airplanes, and chemical weapons not only changed how battles were fought but also transformed military strategy and the experience of soldiers on the front lines. As a result, WWI served as a harbinger of modern warfare, foreshadowing the complexities and moral dilemmas that would define conflicts in the 20th century and beyond. The lessons learned from these technological advancements continue to resonate in contemporary military strategies, making the Great War a critical study in the evolution of warfare.

The Global Impact of World War I

World War I, often referred to as the Great War, had profound implications that extended far beyond the battlefields of Europe. The conflict, which lasted from 1914 to 1918, not only redefined national boundaries and altered the political landscape of Europe but also had significant repercussions on colonies and countries around the world. This global impact can be understood through various dimensions, including economic transformations, shifts in colonial governance, and the emergence of nationalist movements.

Economic Transformations

The war fundamentally reshaped economies on a global scale. European powers, heavily reliant on their colonies for resources and manpower, directed vast amounts of resources towards the war effort. This economic mobilization often resulted in increased production demands in colonies, leading to the exploitation of natural resources at unprecedented levels. For instance, in Africa, countries like Nigeria and South Africa saw enhanced agricultural and mineral extraction activities, which were critical to supporting the war.

However, this economic focus also had negative repercussions. Post-war, many colonies faced economic instability as they struggled with the transition from wartime production to peacetime economies. The influx of war-related infrastructure investments, such as railways and ports, left behind a dual legacy: while they improved connectivity, they also entrenched colonial economic structures that favored imperial powers over local development. Additionally, the war led to inflation and food shortages in many colonies, exacerbating local grievances against colonial authorities.

Shifts in Colonial Governance

World War I also prompted significant changes in the governance of colonies. The war's demands necessitated greater involvement of colonial subjects in governance and military service, leading to a gradual erosion of traditional colonial hierarchies. In many cases, colonial powers recruited soldiers from their colonies, granting them greater political visibility and a sense of agency. For instance, troops from India, Africa, and the Caribbean served in significant numbers, and their contributions were acknowledged in various ways, albeit often insufficiently.

Moreover, the end of the war saw the emergence of the League of Nations, which, despite its limitations, provided a platform for discussing colonial issues on a global stage. The principles of self-determination espoused by leaders like U.S. President Woodrow Wilson resonated with nationalist movements in colonies, sparking demands for independence and self-governance. This ideological shift laid the groundwork for future decolonization movements, as colonies began to question the legitimacy of imperial rule.

Emergence of Nationalist Movements
The fallout from World War I ignited nationalist sentiments across various regions. In Asia, for example, the war catalyzed movements for independence. The Indian National Congress, which had been advocating for greater self-governance prior to the war, gained momentum as returning soldiers and war veterans began to demand political rights and reform. Similarly, in the Middle East, the dissolution of the Ottoman Empire and the subsequent division of its territories fueled aspirations for national identity and self-rule, leading to profound geopolitical changes.

In Africa, the war served as a catalyst for the growth of nationalist movements, as leaders began to articulate the need for self-determination and independence. The experiences of African soldiers during the war fostered a sense of pride and agency, which would later contribute to the rise of independence movements across the continent in the decades that followed.

Conclusion
In conclusion, World War I had a far-reaching impact on colonies and countries beyond Europe, catalyzing economic changes, altering governance structures, and fostering nationalist movements. The legacies of the Great War laid the groundwork for significant political transformations in the interwar period and the eventual wave of decolonization that swept through the 20th century. As the world grappled with the aftermath of the war, the reverberations of this global conflict continued to shape international relations, colonial dynamics, and national identities long into the future.

The Treaty of Versailles and Its Consequences
The Treaty of Versailles, signed on June 28, 1919, marked the official conclusion of World War I, a cataclysmic conflict that had engulfed much of Europe and beyond. The treaty was the result of extensive negotiations among the Allied powers, primarily led by the United States, France, and the United Kingdom, and was aimed at establishing a new order to prevent further large-scale wars. However, the terms of the treaty and their implementation sowed the seeds for future conflicts, particularly World War II.

One of the most significant aspects of the Treaty of Versailles was its punitive approach towards Germany, which was held responsible for the war. The treaty imposed harsh reparations on Germany, requiring it to pay 132 billion gold marks (approximately $33 billion at the time) to the Allied nations. This enormous financial burden devastated the German economy, leading to hyperinflation and widespread poverty in the 1920s. The economic turmoil created fertile ground for political extremism, as many Germans sought scapegoats for their suffering, ultimately leading to the rise of Adolf Hitler and the Nazi Party.

In addition to reparations, the treaty mandated significant territorial losses for Germany. The provinces of Alsace and Lorraine were returned to France, while territories in the east were ceded to Poland, and the Saar Basin was placed under the administration of the League of Nations. The loss of these territories not only diminished Germany's economic resources but also fostered a sense of humiliation and resentment among its populace. The treaty's provisions effectively stripped Germany of its status as a great power, creating a nationalistic fervor that would later manifest in aggressive expansionism.

The treaty also established the League of Nations, an international organization intended to promote peace and cooperation among nations. While the League had noble aspirations, it ultimately proved ineffective in preventing future conflicts. One of the main reasons for this failure was the absence of the United States, which, despite being a principal architect of the League, never ratified the Treaty of Versailles due to a reluctance among American politicians to entangle the country in European affairs. The League's inability to enforce its resolutions further undermined its credibility, as demonstrated by its impotence in the face of Japanese aggression in Manchuria and Italian expansion in Ethiopia.

Moreover, the Treaty of Versailles failed to address the underlying issues that had fueled the war, such as nationalism and imperialism. The redrawing of borders in Central and Eastern Europe, which sought to create nation-states based on ethnic identities, often disregarded historical, cultural, and social realities. This led to ethnic tensions and conflicts in regions like the Balkans and Eastern Europe, laying the groundwork for future instability.

In summary, while the Treaty of Versailles aimed to bring about peace and prevent future wars, its punitive measures against Germany, the failure of the League of Nations, and the mishandling of national boundaries contributed to a volatile international environment. The repercussions of the treaty would not only haunt Europe throughout the interwar years but also play a pivotal role in the outbreak of World War II. The treaty serves as a cautionary tale about the complexities of peace settlements and the importance of addressing the root causes of conflict rather than merely punishing the aggressors.

Chapter 10

World War II

The Rise of Fascism and the Road to War

The interwar period, spanning from the end of World War I in 1918 to the onset of World War II in 1939, was marked by significant political, economic, and social upheaval. The harsh realities of the Treaty of Versailles, which concluded WWI, sowed the seeds of discontent in several nations, particularly Germany. The treaty imposed punitive reparations, territorial losses, and military restrictions on the defeated Central Powers, fostering a sense of humiliation and resentment that would later be exploited by extremist political movements.

In Germany, the Weimar Republic struggled to establish itself amidst a backdrop of economic instability, hyperinflation, and political extremism. The economic crisis of the early 1920s devastated the middle class, eroding support for democratic institutions. As discontent grew, radical ideologies gained traction. Among these, fascism emerged as a potent political force, advocating for authoritarianism, nationalism, and militarism.

Fascism found its most notorious expression in Mussolini's Italy, where Benito Mussolini capitalized on national dissatisfaction. The Italian Fascist Party promised to restore Italy to its former glory, emphasizing a revival of nationalism and a return to traditional values. Mussolini's regime employed propaganda, censorship, and violent suppression of opposition to consolidate power, establishing a template for future fascist movements.

In Germany, Adolf Hitler and the National Socialist German Workers' Party (NSDAP) similarly rose to prominence by exploiting the fears and frustrations of the populace. Hitler's oratory skills and charismatic leadership captivated many Germans who were disillusioned with the Weimar government. The Nazi Party's platform promised economic revival, national rejuvenation, and the expansion of German territory, resonating deeply with a society battered by war and economic strife. Central to Hitler's ideology was a virulent form of nationalism intertwined with racist doctrines, particularly anti-Semitism, which scapegoated Jewish people for Germany's woes.

The global context of the 1920s and 1930s also contributed to the rise of fascism. The Great Depression, which began in 1929, triggered economic crises worldwide, exacerbating political instability. Countries across Europe faced unemployment, poverty, and social unrest, leading many to seek radical solutions. Fascism's promises of order, discipline, and national pride became increasingly appealing in such turbulent times.

The failure of democratic governments to address these crises allowed fascist parties to gain ground. In Spain, the rise of Francisco Franco and the onset of the Spanish Civil War (1936-1939) reflected the broader conflict between fascism and leftist ideologies. Franco's eventual victory, supported by Nazi Germany and Fascist Italy, demonstrated the growing influence and collaboration of fascist regimes in Europe.

The international response to the rise of fascism was characterized by a policy of appeasement, particularly from Britain and France. This approach aimed to avoid conflict by conceding to some of the demands of aggressive powers, such as Hitler's reoccupation of the Rhineland and the annexation of Austria. However, these concessions only emboldened fascist ambitions, culminating in the invasion of Poland in September 1939, which triggered World War II.

In summary, the rise of fascism and the road to global conflict were shaped by a complex interplay of political ideologies, economic despair, and national grievances following World War I. The inability of democratic systems to respond effectively to these challenges allowed authoritarian regimes to flourish, ultimately leading to one of the deadliest conflicts in human history. The lessons learned from this era underscore the importance of addressing societal grievances and fostering inclusive political systems to prevent the resurgence of such ideologies.

Major Theaters of War in World War II

World War II was characterized by its unprecedented scale and complexity, encompassing multiple theaters of conflict that spanned continents and involved numerous nations. The major theaters of war included Europe, the Pacific, and North Africa, each presenting unique challenges, strategies, and outcomes that collectively shaped the course of the global conflict.

Europe

The European theater was the primary front of World War II, marked by a sequence of significant campaigns and battles that defined the conflict. The war in Europe began with the German invasion of Poland in September 1939, which prompted Britain and France to declare war on Germany. The early years saw rapid German advances, with the Blitzkrieg tactics allowing for swift victories over countries like France and the Low Countries in 1940.

The turning point in Europe came with Operation Barbarossa, Hitler's ill-fated invasion of the Soviet Union in June 1941. This opened a brutal Eastern Front, where two of the largest and deadliest battles of the war occurred: the Battle of Stalingrad (1942-1943) and the Siege of Leningrad (1941-1944). The harsh winter, combined with fierce Soviet resistance, eventually led to a significant shift in momentum towards the Allies.

By 1944, with the D-Day landings in Normandy (Operation Overlord), Allied forces began a concerted effort to liberate Western Europe. The subsequent liberation of France and the push into Germany culminated in the unconditional surrender of Nazi Germany in May 1945, marking a decisive victory for the Allies in Europe.

The Pacific

The Pacific theater of World War II was characterized by a series of naval battles and island-hopping campaigns as the United States sought to defeat Japan after the attack on Pearl Harbor in December 1941. The early stages of the war saw rapid Japanese expansions, claiming territories across Southeast Asia and the Pacific Islands.

Significant battles in this theater included the Battle of Midway (June 1942), which marked a turning point as American forces decisively defeated the Japanese navy, shifting the balance of power in the Pacific. The island-hopping strategy, employed by General Douglas MacArthur and Admiral Chester W. Nimitz, aimed to capture strategically important islands while bypassing heavily fortified ones, allowing Allied forces to move closer to Japan.

The war reached its climax with the brutal battles of Iwo Jima (February-March 1945) and Okinawa (April-June 1945), which resulted in heavy casualties on both sides and demonstrated Japan's fierce determination to fight to the bitter end. The Pacific theater concluded with the dropping of atomic bombs on Hiroshima and Nagasaki in August 1945, leading to Japan's surrender and the end of World War II.

North Africa

The North African theater was crucial in the fight against Axis powers, particularly Germany and Italy. The conflict began in 1940 with the Italian invasion of Egypt and quickly escalated with the German Afrika Korps, led by General Erwin Rommel. The battles of El Alamein (1942) marked a significant turning point, as British forces under General Bernard Montgomery halted the Axis advance.

The campaign in North Africa was characterized by a series of back-and-forth engagements, with control over the Suez Canal and access to Middle Eastern oil being primary objectives. The eventual Allied victory in North Africa laid the groundwork for the Italian Campaign, as Allied forces invaded Sicily in 1943, ultimately leading to the downfall of Mussolini's regime.

Beyond the Major Theaters
While Europe, the Pacific, and North Africa were the primary theaters of war, conflicts also erupted in other regions, including Southeast Asia and the Arctic, involving diverse military operations and strategies. Each theater played a vital role in the overall dynamics of World War II, influencing not only military strategies but also the post-war geopolitical landscape.

The complexity and interconnectivity of these theaters illustrate the global nature of World War II, with each front contributing to the eventual defeat of the Axis powers and the reshaping of international relations in the subsequent decades. The lessons learned from these theaters continue to inform military strategy and international policy today.

The Holocaust and War Crimes

The Holocaust stands as one of the most horrific chapters in human history, representing the systematic genocide of six million Jews and millions of others deemed "undesirable" by the Nazi regime, including Romani people, disabled individuals, Polish citizens, Soviet prisoners of war, and political dissidents. This atrocity unfolded during World War II, a conflict marked not only by military engagements but also by a chilling campaign of extermination that sought to eliminate entire populations.

The roots of the Holocaust lay in centuries of deep-seated anti-Semitism in Europe, exacerbated by the economic turmoil and political instability following World War I. Adolf Hitler and the Nazi Party exploited these sentiments, promoting an ideology that blamed Jews for Germany's struggles and portrayed them as a threat to the so-called Aryan race. Following Hitler's rise to power in 1933, discriminatory laws were enacted, stripping Jews of their rights and social standing. The Nuremberg Laws of 1935 institutionalized racial discrimination, segregating Jews from the broader society and paving the way for more extreme measures.

The onset of World War II in 1939 provided the Nazi regime with the cover and means to escalate their campaign of persecution. As German forces invaded Poland, they established ghettos to confine Jewish populations, subjecting them to starvation, disease, and brutal treatment. The mass shootings by Einsatzgruppen (mobile killing units) marked the beginning of what would become the industrialized genocide known as the Holocaust. By 1941, the Nazis had implemented the "Final Solution," a systematic plan for the extermination of Jews in concentration and extermination camps.

Camps such as Auschwitz, Treblinka, and Sobibor became notorious for their horrific conditions and mass murder through gas chambers and forced labor. The scale of the atrocities was unprecedented; millions were subjected to inhumane conditions, medical experimentation, and executed in mass killings. The Holocaust not only decimated Jewish communities across Europe but also left a profound psychological and cultural scar that would resonate for generations.

The impact of the Holocaust extended beyond the immediate loss of life and destruction of communities. It fundamentally changed the global understanding of human rights and the need for accountability in the face of atrocities. The sheer scale and brutality of the Holocaust led to a reevaluation of ethical standards regarding warfare and human dignity. In its aftermath, the Nuremberg Trials were established to prosecute key Nazi leaders for war crimes, crimes against humanity, and genocide. These trials set a precedent for international law and established the principle that individuals, including heads of state, could be held accountable for their actions during war.

The Holocaust also spurred the establishment of the United Nations and the Universal Declaration of Human Rights in 1948, reflecting a global commitment to prevent such atrocities from occurring in the future. However, the legacy of the Holocaust is complex; it serves as a reminder of the depths of human cruelty and the necessity of vigilance in protecting human rights. The ongoing struggle against anti-Semitism and discrimination underscores the need for education, remembrance, and commitment to the principles of tolerance and justice.

In conclusion, the Holocaust was not merely a historical event but a harrowing lesson on the consequences of hatred, intolerance, and indifference. Its impact continues to shape contemporary discussions about war crimes, human rights, and the moral responsibilities of nations and individuals in preventing future atrocities. As societies reflect on this dark chapter, the imperative remains clear: to remember, to educate, and to ensure that such horrors are never repeated.

The Role of Allied Leaders in World War II

World War II was a global conflict that spanned from 1939 to 1945, involving many nations and resulting in unprecedented devastation. Central to the Allied victory were the influential leaders who navigated the complex geopolitical landscape of the time. Among these, Winston Churchill, Franklin D. Roosevelt, and Joseph Stalin played pivotal roles, each contributing uniquely to the war's strategy, diplomacy, and ultimate outcome.

Winston Churchill: The Resolute Visionary

Winston Churchill became the British Prime Minister in May 1940, during one of the darkest hours of World War II. His leadership was characterized by steadfast resolve and an unyielding spirit, which inspired not only the British people but also the broader Allied forces. Churchill's speeches, imbued with a sense of urgency and determination, rallied the nation during the Blitz, fostering a sense of unity and resilience against Nazi aggression.

Churchill was also instrumental in forging critical alliances. Recognizing the need for collaboration, he worked closely with Roosevelt, establishing a strong Anglo-American partnership. This partnership was crucial for coordinating military strategies and economic support. The Atlantic Charter, drafted by Churchill and Roosevelt in August 1941, laid the groundwork for post-war cooperation and articulated shared goals for a world free from tyranny. Churchill's strategic acumen was evident in key military decisions, including the prioritization of the North African campaign and the planning of the D-Day invasion, which ultimately turned the tide against the Axis powers.

Franklin D. Roosevelt: The Architect of Allied Strategy

Franklin D. Roosevelt, the President of the United States, played a critical role in mobilizing American resources for the war effort. Roosevelt's initial strategy focused on supporting the Allies through programs such as Lend-Lease, which provided critical military supplies to nations like Britain and the Soviet Union before the U.S. formally entered the war in December 1941. His foresight in recognizing the threat posed by Axis powers and his commitment to supporting Allied nations were vital in sustaining the fight against fascism.

Roosevelt was also a master of diplomacy. He effectively managed tensions among the Allies, particularly between Churchill and Stalin. His participation in the Tehran Conference in 1943 exemplified his diplomatic skills as he worked to ensure cooperation among the Big Three—Britain, the United States, and the Soviet Union. Roosevelt's ability to maintain a cohesive Allied front was instrumental in orchestrating joint military operations and establishing a unified command structure, which was essential for successful campaigns in Europe and the Pacific.

Joseph Stalin: The Resilient Commander

Joseph Stalin, the leader of the Soviet Union, represented a different facet of leadership during World War II. Following the initial setbacks suffered by the Red Army due to the German invasion in June 1941, Stalin's resolve became evident. He rallied the Soviet populace and military, emphasizing the existential threat posed by Nazi Germany. The resilience demonstrated during the brutal Siege of Leningrad and the pivotal Battle of Stalingrad marked turning points in the war, showcasing the Soviet Union's capacity to absorb and eventually repel the German onslaught.

Stalin's leadership was marked by a willingness to engage in brutal tactics to achieve military objectives. His commitment to the war effort resulted in significant sacrifices, but it also led to the Soviet Union emerging as a superpower post-war. Stalin's collaboration with Churchill and Roosevelt, particularly at the Yalta Conference, played a crucial role in shaping the post-war order in Europe, although it also set the stage for future geopolitical tensions during the Cold War.

Conclusion

The contributions of Churchill, Roosevelt, and Stalin were instrumental in the Allied victory in World War II. Their distinct leadership styles, forged through the crucible of conflict, not only influenced military strategies but also shaped the international relations landscape of the post-war world. Their ability to work together, despite ideological differences and national interests, was crucial in overcoming the Axis powers and establishing a foundation for future global cooperation, albeit one that would be tested in the ensuing Cold War. The legacy of these leaders is a testament to the critical impact of political will and strategic vision in times of global crisis.

The Aftermath of WWII

The conclusion of World War II in 1945 marked a pivotal moment in global history, resulting in profound changes that reshaped the political landscape of Europe and the world. The war, which had caused unprecedented destruction and loss of life, ended with the Allied powers emerging triumphant but faced with the daunting challenge of rebuilding a war-torn world. The aftermath of WWII can be characterized by the division of Europe, the establishment of the United Nations, and the onset of the Cold War, each of which set the stage for geopolitical tensions that would define the latter half of the 20th century.

The Division of Europe

The most immediate consequence of WWII was the division of Europe into spheres of influence dominated by the victorious powers. The Yalta and Potsdam Conferences, held in 1945, laid the groundwork for this division. The leaders of the United States, the United Kingdom, and the Soviet Union negotiated the postwar order, resulting in the partitioning of Germany and the creation of Eastern and Western blocs. Germany was split into four occupation zones controlled by the US, the UK, France, and the Soviet Union. Berlin, located deep within the Soviet zone, was similarly divided, setting the stage for future conflicts.

In Eastern Europe, the Soviet Union installed communist governments, effectively turning countries like Poland, Hungary, and Czechoslovakia into satellite states. The Iron Curtain, a term popularized by Winston Churchill, symbolized this division, marking a clear demarcation between the capitalist West and the communist East. This division not only reflected ideological differences but also led to significant political, economic, and social ramifications for the nations involved.

The Creation of the United Nations

In response to the devastation of WWII and a shared desire to prevent future global conflicts, the United Nations (UN) was established in October 1945. The UN aimed to promote international cooperation, peace, and security, providing a platform for dialogue among nations. The founding charter emphasized the importance of human rights, economic development, and social progress.

The UN became instrumental in addressing postwar challenges, including humanitarian crises, refugee resettlement, and the rebuilding of war-torn nations. Agencies such as the United Nations Relief and Works Agency (UNRWA) and the United Nations Educational, Scientific and Cultural Organization (UNESCO) were created to tackle specific issues arising from the war. However, the UN's effectiveness was often hampered by the ideological rift between the US and the Soviet Union, which influenced its operations and decision-making processes.

The Start of the Cold War

The ideological clash between capitalism and communism soon escalated into the Cold War, a prolonged period of geopolitical tension between the United States and the Soviet Union. The emergence of nuclear weapons, coupled with the arms race, heightened fears of a direct military confrontation. Events such as the Berlin Blockade in 1948-1949 and the establishment of NATO in 1949 exemplified the growing antagonism.

The Cold War was characterized by various proxy wars, espionage, and competition for global influence. The US and its allies sought to contain the spread of communism, leading to interventions in places like Korea and Vietnam, while the Soviet Union aimed to expand its influence in Asia, Africa, and Latin America. The ideological, military, and economic rivalry between the two superpowers shaped international relations for decades, influencing everything from foreign policy to cultural exchanges.

Conclusion

The aftermath of WWII was a complex tapestry of division, cooperation, and conflict. The division of Europe created a stark ideological divide that would dominate global politics for much of the 20th century. The establishment of the UN illustrated a concerted effort to foster international collaboration and prevent future wars, despite the challenges posed by the Cold War. As nations navigated their postwar realities, the legacies of WWII continued to resonate, shaping the course of history and influencing the nature of conflicts for generations to come.

Chapter 11

The Korean War

The Origins of the Korean Conflict

The Korean War, which erupted in June 1950, is one of the pivotal conflicts of the 20th century, rooted deeply in the geopolitical and ideological struggles that emerged in the aftermath of World War II. The origins of the Korean conflict can be traced back to the division of Korea at the end of the war, which set the stage for one of the first major confrontations of the Cold War.

At the conclusion of World War II in 1945, Korea was liberated from Japanese colonial rule, which had lasted for 35 years. However, the liberation was soon overshadowed by the competing interests of the United States and the Soviet Union, the two superpowers that emerged from the war with significantly contrasting ideologies. The Korean Peninsula was divided along the 38th parallel, with the Soviet Union occupying the northern part and the United States taking control of the southern part. This division was supposed to be temporary, intended to facilitate the disarmament of Japanese troops and the eventual reunification of Korea. However, the growing tensions of the Cold War led to the establishment of two distinct governments: the Democratic People's Republic of Korea (North Korea) in the north, supported by the Soviet Union and China, and the Republic of Korea (South Korea) in the south, backed by the United States and its Western allies.

The ideological divide between the two Koreas could not have been more pronounced. North Korea, under the leadership of Kim Il-sung, embraced a communist system, seeking to implement land reforms and collectivization inspired by Soviet models. In contrast, South Korea, led by Syngman Rhee, adopted a capitalist framework, promoting democratic governance, albeit in a manner that often suppressed dissent and opposition.

By the late 1940s, both regimes began to solidify their power, and the Korean Peninsula became increasingly polarized. Propaganda campaigns intensified, each side portraying the other as a direct threat to its sovereignty and ideology. The escalating tensions were exacerbated by border skirmishes along the 38th parallel, where incursions and military clashes became common as each side sought to assert dominance.

The situation took a dramatic turn on June 25, 1950, when North Korean forces launched a surprise invasion into South Korea. This act of aggression was motivated by Kim Il-sung's belief that a military solution was necessary to reunify Korea under communist rule. With the support of the Soviet Union and tacit approval from Mao Zedong of China, North Korea aimed to quickly overwhelm the unprepared South. The swift advance of North Korean troops led to the capture of Seoul within days, prompting an urgent response from the United States and the United Nations.

In response to the invasion, U.S. President Harry S. Truman ordered American military forces to assist South Korea. This marked the beginning of a significant military engagement, with the United Nations subsequently approving a multinational force to repel the North Korean aggression. The Korean War thus transformed from a civil conflict into a proxy war, with both superpowers heavily invested in the outcome.

The origins of the Korean conflict reveal the complexities of post-war geopolitics, the impact of colonial legacies, and the fierce ideological battles that characterized the Cold War. The division of Korea not only precipitated a devastating war but also set the stage for decades of tension, militarization, and division that continue to resonate in the region today. The Korean War ultimately became a crucial moment in history, shaping the dynamics of international relations and the Cold War landscape for years to come.

Major Battles and Military Strategies in the Korean War

The Korean War (1950-1953) was marked by a series of significant battles and strategic maneuvers that defined its course. Among the most pivotal events were the Inchon Landing, the Chinese intervention, and several key military engagements that shaped the conflict's dynamics.

Inchon Landing

The Inchon Landing, executed on September 15, 1950, was a daring amphibious assault led by General Douglas MacArthur. The objective was to retake Seoul and cut off North Korean supply lines, which had been pushing southward since their invasion of South Korea in June 1950. The choice of Inchon, a port city situated far behind enemy lines, was bold due to its challenging tides and fortified positions. However, MacArthur's gamble paid off; the landing caught North Korean forces by surprise, leading to a rapid advance. Within weeks, United Nations (UN) forces recaptured Seoul, significantly altering the war's momentum and allowing the chase of retreating North Korean troops toward the 38th parallel.

Chinese Intervention

However, the success at Inchon triggered a critical response from China. As UN forces advanced northward, nearing the Yalu River, the Chinese government perceived the threat to their borders and intervened decisively. On October 19, 1950, the People's Volunteer Army crossed into Korea, significantly outnumbering UN forces. The Chinese strategy relied on the element of surprise and overwhelming numbers, launching a series of assaults that pushed the UN troops back to the south. This intervention marked a turning point in the war, leading to a protracted stalemate and a redefined front line.

Major Battles

Several key battles characterized the conflict following the Chinese intervention. The Battle of Chosin Reservoir (November-December 1950) stands out as one of the most brutal engagements. UN forces, predominantly U.S. Marines, found themselves encircled by Chinese troops during a harsh winter. The fighting was fierce, with UN forces exhibiting remarkable resilience as they conducted a fighting withdrawal over difficult terrain, retreating to the port of Hungnam. The battle revealed the tenacity of both sides and underscored the harsh conditions of the conflict.

Another significant engagement was the Battle of Pusan Perimeter (August-September 1950). When North Korean forces initially invaded, they pushed UN troops into a small perimeter around the city of Pusan. Here, UN forces established a defensive line that ultimately held against the North Korean advance. The successful defense at Pusan was crucial in maintaining a foothold in Korea and set the stage for the subsequent counter-offensive at Inchon.

Military Strategies

Throughout the Korean War, military strategies evolved in response to the shifting dynamics of the battlefield. The UN command, under MacArthur, initially focused on rapid offensive maneuvers and reclaiming lost territory. However, as the war progressed and with the Chinese intervention, strategies adapted to incorporate more defensive postures and guerrilla tactics. The introduction of air power was also significant, with air superiority becoming a crucial factor in both offensive and defensive operations.

Moreover, the use of intelligence and reconnaissance played a vital role, as both sides sought to understand and anticipate each other's movements. The harsh terrain of Korea, combined with the unpredictable weather, often influenced tactical decisions, leading to innovative approaches, including night assaults and the use of artillery barrages.

In conclusion, the major battles and military strategies of the Korean War reflect the complexities of modern warfare, emphasizing the interplay of bold maneuvers, international politics, and the harsh realities of combat. The outcomes of these engagements not only shaped the course of the war but also laid the groundwork for the geopolitical landscape of East Asia in the subsequent decades.

The Role of International Powers in the Korean War

The Korean War (1950-1953) stands as a pivotal conflict in the history of the 20th century, emblematic of the broader ideological struggle between communism and capitalism that defined the Cold War era. The involvement of international powers like the United States, China, the Soviet Union, and the United Nations significantly influenced the conflict's dynamics, strategies, and ultimately its outcome.

United States: A Commitment to Containment

The United States viewed the Korean War as a critical front in its broader strategy of containment against the spread of communism. Following World War II, Korea was divided along the 38th parallel into two separate states: the communist North, backed by the Soviet Union and China, and the capitalist South, supported by the United States and its allies. The U.S. leadership believed that if Korea fell to communism, a domino effect could ensue, threatening other nations in Asia. Thus, when North Korea invaded South Korea in June 1950, President Harry S. Truman quickly committed U.S. military forces to repel the invasion under the auspices of the United Nations.

The U.S. not only provided troops but also extensive military resources and strategic planning, including the daring Inchon Landing, which turned the tide in favor of UN forces. The American involvement was marked by a significant escalation of military engagement, leading to a push northward towards the Chinese border.

Soviet Union: A Calculated Support for the North

The Soviet Union played a dual role during the Korean War. Initially, it supported the North Korean regime of Kim Il-sung through military aid, equipment, and strategic advice. The Soviets viewed Korea as an opportunity to expand their influence in Asia and counter U.S. presence. At the onset of the war, Joseph Stalin provided tacit approval for Kim's invasion, believing that the U.S. would not intervene.

As the conflict escalated, the Soviet Union continued to supply North Korea with resources and military hardware, including aircraft and artillery, which helped sustain the North's war effort. However, the Soviets were cautious about direct military involvement, wary of provoking a broader conflict with the U.S. and its allies.

China: The Intervention of the People's Republic
China's involvement in the Korean War marked a decisive turning point. Following the initial success of UN forces pushing towards the Yalu River, the Chinese government, under Mao Zedong, perceived a direct threat to its national security. In October 1950, China entered the war with a massive volunteer army, known as the People's Volunteer Army (PVA), launching surprise offensives that overwhelmed UN forces and pushed them back into South Korea.

China's intervention was crucial in stabilizing the North Korean front, and it underscored the deep geopolitical interests at play. The Chinese leadership sought not only to safeguard its border but also to assert itself as a formidable power in Asia and counter U.S. influence in the region.

United Nations: A Multinational Response
The United Nations played an essential role in the Korean War, marking one of the first instances of collective military action under its auspices. In response to North Korea's aggression, the UN Security Council quickly passed resolutions calling for member states to assist South Korea. This led to a multinational force, predominantly composed of U.S. troops, but also involving soldiers from other nations, including the United Kingdom, Canada, and Australia.

The UN's involvement provided a framework for international legitimacy and support for the war effort. However, the varying motivations of the member states reflected the complexities of Cold War politics, with countries participating for diverse reasons—some out of ideological alignment with the West, others due to obligations to international cooperation.

Conclusion
The Korean War epitomized the intricate interplay of international powers during the Cold War, where decisions shaped by ideological commitments, national security concerns, and global politics converged on the Korean Peninsula. The consequences of this conflict were profound, not only for Korea but also for the geopolitical landscape of the 20th century, setting the stage for ongoing tensions in the region and influencing international relations for decades to come.

The Armistice and Its Aftermath
The Korean War, which erupted in 1950, was a complex and multifaceted conflict primarily involving North Korea, supported by China and the Soviet Union, and South Korea, backed by the United Nations forces led by the United States. After three years of intense fighting, the war came to a halt with the signing of an armistice on July 27, 1953. This agreement effectively ceased hostilities but did not result in a formal peace treaty, leaving the Korean Peninsula in a state of unresolved tension that persists to this day.

The armistice was negotiated at Panmunjom, a village located within the Korean Demilitarized Zone (DMZ), which became a buffer zone between the two Koreas. The negotiations were fraught with difficulties, as both sides held starkly different visions for the future of Korea. North Korea and its allies sought to unify the peninsula under a communist regime, while the South, supported by the U.S. and other Western nations, aimed to maintain a separate, democratic government. The armistice ultimately established a ceasefire and created the DMZ, which remains one of the most militarized borders in the world.

The terms of the armistice included the withdrawal of all foreign troops from Korea, the establishment of the DMZ, and the return of prisoners of war. However, the document itself was not a peace treaty, which meant that the two Koreas technically remained in a state of war. The absence of a formal peace agreement has left a legacy of mutual suspicion and hostility, fueling ongoing military confrontations and diplomatic standoffs.

In the immediate aftermath of the armistice, the Korean Peninsula was left divided along the 38th parallel, with North Korea under the leadership of Kim Il-sung and South Korea led by Syngman Rhee. The DMZ became a stark physical and ideological barrier, symbolizing the broader Cold War division between communism and capitalism. There were significant humanitarian consequences as families were torn apart, with many individuals unable to reunite with loved ones on the other side of the border.

Over the decades, the relationship between North and South Korea has been marked by episodes of heightened tension, military provocations, and sporadic attempts at dialogue. North Korea's pursuit of nuclear weapons has further complicated the situation, leading to international sanctions and increased military readiness in the South. The South Korean government has oscillated between hardline policies and engagement strategies, reflecting the challenges of navigating inter-Korean relations while considering the influence of external powers, particularly the U.S. and China.

The legacy of the armistice is evident in contemporary issues such as the ongoing military presence of U.S. forces in South Korea, the frequent military drills conducted by both North and South Korea, and the repeated North Korean provocations, including missile tests. The DMZ remains a potent symbol of division, attracting attention from tourists and researchers alike, while also serving as a reminder of the unresolved conflict.

In conclusion, the armistice that ended hostilities in the Korean War did not bring about a lasting peace; instead, it institutionalized a division that continues to shape the geopolitical landscape of East Asia. The ongoing tensions and the lack of a formal peace treaty highlight the complexities of achieving reconciliation on the Korean Peninsula, as both Koreas navigate their distinct identities and historical grievances in an ever-evolving global context. The legacy of the Korean War and its aftermath continues to influence regional dynamics, making the pursuit of peace and stability a critical issue for future generations.

The Legacy of the Korean War

The Korean War, which lasted from 1950 to 1953, left a profound legacy that continues to influence international relations and the geopolitical landscape of East Asia. Its ramifications were particularly significant within the context of the Cold War, shaping the dynamics between major powers and the future of the Korean Peninsula.

Cold War Dynamics

The Korean War was a pivotal event in the Cold War, marking the first significant military conflict between the forces of communism and capitalism after World War II. The war solidified the division of the world into two opposing blocs: the communist bloc led by the Soviet Union and China, and the capitalist bloc spearheaded by the United States and its allies. The involvement of international powers in the conflict underscored the global stakes of the Cold War, as the United States perceived the invasion of South Korea by North Korean forces as a test of its resolve against the spread of communism.

Furthermore, the war set a precedent for U.S. military intervention in conflicts around the globe under the doctrine of containment. This policy aimed to prevent the expansion of communism and justified U.S. involvement in various regional conflicts, including those in Vietnam and elsewhere in Asia, the Middle East, and Latin America. The United Nations' involvement, with a coalition of forces predominantly led by the United States, also established a framework for collective security that would be invoked in future conflicts.

The Korean Peninsula: A Divided Nation

The armistice that ended hostilities in 1953 effectively cemented the division of Korea along the 38th parallel, creating two distinct nations: North Korea (officially the Democratic People's Republic of Korea) and South Korea (the Republic of Korea). This division was not merely geographical but ideological, as the two Koreas adopted starkly different political systems, economies, and social structures. North Korea became an isolated, authoritarian state with a centrally planned economy, heavily relying on military spending and allegiance to its ruling dynasty. In contrast, South Korea developed into a vibrant democracy with a market-oriented economy, benefitting from U.S. support and investment.

The legacy of the Korean War is reflected in the ongoing tensions and hostilities between the two Koreas. The Demilitarized Zone (DMZ), established as a buffer between the North and South, remains one of the most fortified borders in the world. Military skirmishes, political provocations, and an enduring arms race have characterized relations since the war's conclusion, perpetuating a climate of fear and uncertainty on the peninsula.

Long-Term Global Implications
Beyond the Korean Peninsula, the legacy of the Korean War has had lasting implications for global stability. It highlighted the potential for localized conflicts to escalate into larger confrontations, a theme that would recur throughout the Cold War. The war also influenced U.S.-China relations, as the Chinese intervention on behalf of North Korea established a precedent for China's role as a key player in regional and global affairs.

Moreover, the Korean War left a lasting impact on military strategy and international relations. The concept of "limited war" emerged, where nations would engage in conflict without fully committing to total war, a strategy that would be evident in subsequent conflicts. The war also prompted a reevaluation of nuclear deterrence and the need for military preparedness, influencing defense policies for decades.

Conclusion
In summary, the legacy of the Korean War is multifaceted, shaping Cold War dynamics and leaving an indelible mark on the Korean Peninsula. The division of Korea remains a crucial point of contention in East Asian geopolitics, and the conflict's historical lessons continue to resonate in contemporary discussions about international security, military strategy, and the pursuit of peace. The war serves as a reminder of the complex interplay between local conflicts and global power dynamics, highlighting the enduring struggle for stability and resolution in a divided world.

Chapter 12

The Vietnam War

The Origins of the Vietnam Conflict

The Vietnam Conflict, often referred to as the Vietnam War, did not emerge in isolation but rather stemmed from a complex interplay of historical, political, and social factors that began with French colonial rule in Indochina. The late 19th century marked the establishment of French colonial dominance over Vietnam, Laos, and Cambodia, collectively known as French Indochina. This period was characterized by economic exploitation, cultural suppression, and a systematic dismantling of local governance. The imposition of French culture and Catholicism, coupled with the extraction of resources, fostered resentment among the Vietnamese populace.

The French colonial legacy laid the groundwork for significant nationalistic movements. By the early 20th century, intellectuals and nationalists began to emerge, advocating for independence from colonial rule. Figures such as Ho Chi Minh, who would later become a central figure in the fight against both colonialism and, subsequently, American intervention, began to rally support for independence. Ho Chi Minh's journey through France and his exposure to socialist and communist ideologies deeply influenced his political outlook, which would later play a pivotal role in shaping the struggle for Vietnamese autonomy.

The socio-economic structures established by the French further exacerbated class divisions and regional disparities. The land reforms introduced by the French largely favored wealthy landowners and marginalized the peasantry, leading to widespread poverty and discontent in the rural areas. This discontent became fertile ground for the spread of communist ideology, as many peasants found the promises of equality and land reform under communism appealing. The rise of the Indochinese Communist Party (ICP) in the 1930s indicated a growing commitment to revolutionary change and the end of colonial rule.

The decline of French colonial power during World War II, especially following the Japanese occupation of Vietnam, created a power vacuum that various nationalist movements sought to fill. The Viet Minh, a communist-led national liberation movement, capitalized on the weakening of French authority and the chaos of the war. Under Ho Chi Minh's leadership, the Viet Minh gained support among the peasantry and urban workers, advocating for independence and social justice, which resonated deeply with a population that had suffered under colonial rule.

Following the end of World War II and Japan's surrender in 1945, the Viet Minh declared Vietnam's independence. However, the French, eager to reestablish their colonial rule, refused to relinquish control, leading to the First Indochina War (1946-1954). This conflict was marked by guerrilla warfare tactics employed by the Viet Minh against French forces, ultimately culminating in the decisive Battle of Dien Bien Phu in 1954, which resulted in a French defeat.

The Geneva Conference that followed divided Vietnam at the 17th parallel, creating North Vietnam, led by the communists under Ho Chi Minh, and South Vietnam, supported by the United States and other Western nations. This division was not merely geographical; it represented contrasting ideologies—communism in the North and a Western-aligned government in the South.

The roots of the Vietnam Conflict can thus be traced back to a legacy of colonial oppression, the rise of nationalist and communist sentiments, and the geopolitical dynamics of the post-World War II era. These elements set the stage for a conflict that would not only engulf Vietnam but also attract global attention, becoming a focal point of Cold War tensions as the United States sought to contain the spread of communism in Southeast Asia. The interplay of these historical forces ultimately defined the trajectory of the Vietnam War, shaping the experiences and the fates of millions.

Major Military Campaigns in the Vietnam War

The Vietnam War, lasting from the late 1950s until 1975, was marked by a series of significant military campaigns that shaped the course of the conflict and its eventual outcome. Among these, the Tet Offensive and Operation Rolling Thunder stand out as pivotal events that not only influenced military strategies but also public perception of the war, both in the United States and Vietnam.

The Tet Offensive (January 1968)

One of the most critical military campaigns of the Vietnam War was the Tet Offensive, launched by the North Vietnamese forces and the Viet Cong during the Vietnamese New Year (Tet) celebrations in January 1968. This offensive was characterized by a series of coordinated surprise attacks on more than 100 cities and military targets across South Vietnam, including the U.S. Embassy in Saigon. The sheer scale and audacity of the Tet Offensive shocked American military and political leaders, as it contradicted their claims that the U.S. was winning the war.

Despite heavy casualties for the North Vietnamese and Viet Cong, the Tet Offensive had profound implications. It exposed vulnerabilities in U.S. and South Vietnamese defenses and severely undermined public confidence in the U.S. government's optimistic narrative about the war. Images of fierce fighting and the chaos of the offensive were broadcast to homes across America, leading to a significant shift in public opinion and increasing calls for de-escalation and withdrawal.

Operation Rolling Thunder (March 1965 - November 1968)
Prior to the Tet Offensive, the U.S. initiated Operation Rolling Thunder, a sustained bombing campaign against North Vietnam that began in March 1965. The operation aimed to weaken the North Vietnamese resolve, disrupt supply lines along the Ho Chi Minh Trail, and bolster the morale of South Vietnamese forces. Over the course of the campaign, the U.S. dropped more bombs on Vietnam than were used during the entirety of World War II.

While Operation Rolling Thunder initially sought to achieve decisive military results, it failed to bring North Vietnam to the negotiating table. The campaign faced challenges, including a lack of clear objectives and the resilience of North Vietnamese forces. Moreover, the extensive bombing resulted in significant civilian casualties and destruction, further alienating the Vietnamese population and fueling anti-war sentiments in the United States.

Other Key Events and Campaigns
In addition to the Tet Offensive and Operation Rolling Thunder, several other military operations played crucial roles in the Vietnam War. The Battle of Khe Sanh (January to July 1968), a protracted siege by North Vietnamese forces, became emblematic of the war's brutality. U.S. Marines were surrounded and besieged, leading to intense fighting and high casualties, ultimately becoming a symbol of the futility of the conflict.

Another significant event was the My Lai Massacre in March 1968, where U.S. soldiers killed hundreds of unarmed Vietnamese civilians. The revelation of this atrocity, alongside other military failures, sparked outrage and intensified anti-war protests across the United States.

Conclusion
The major military campaigns of the Vietnam War, including the Tet Offensive and Operation Rolling Thunder, not only shaped the military landscape of the conflict but also had lasting effects on American society and politics. The shift in public perception, driven by the realities of warfare and the media's role in reporting them, played a significant part in the eventual decision to withdraw U.S. forces from Vietnam. Understanding these campaigns provides crucial insights into the complexities of Vietnam War and its enduring legacy in military history and American consciousness.

The Role of the Media in the Vietnam War

The Vietnam War, fought from the late 1950s until 1975, marked a pivotal moment in history not only for the United States but also for global media and public perception of war. This conflict was unique in that it was the first war extensively covered by television, allowing the gruesome realities of combat to penetrate the living rooms of millions of Americans. The role of media—particularly television and journalism—was crucial in shaping public perception, influencing policy decisions, and mobilizing anti-war sentiments.

The Rise of Television Coverage

Before Vietnam, wars were largely reported through print media, which often filtered information through government channels. However, the Vietnam War introduced a new dynamic with the advent of television as a primary source of news. Graphic images of warfare, including wounded soldiers, civilian casualties, and destruction, were broadcasted in real-time or shortly after events occurred. This immediacy created a visceral connection between the American public and the war, making it difficult to remain detached from the conflict.

Television networks, including CBS, NBC, and ABC, dedicated significant resources to covering the war. Anchors like Walter Cronkite became household names, and their reports played a significant role in shaping public opinion. Cronkite's famous declaration that the war was unwinnable after the Tet Offensive in 1968 marked a turning point, leading many Americans to question the government's optimistic portrayals of progress in Vietnam.

The Impact of Journalism

Journalism during the Vietnam War was characterized by a commitment to investigative reporting. Journalists on the ground, such as David Halberstam and Neil Sheehan, provided unfiltered accounts of the war's realities. Their reports often contradicted official government statements, contributing to a growing skepticism regarding the U.S. government's narrative. The publication of the Pentagon Papers in 1971, which revealed that the government had misled the public about the war's progress, further fueled distrust among the American populace.

The media's role in the Vietnam War was not limited to reporting on the battlefield; it also highlighted the experiences of soldiers and civilians alike. Graphic coverage of the My Lai Massacre, where U.S. troops killed hundreds of unarmed South Vietnamese civilians, sparked outrage and intensified anti-war protests. The emotional weight of such coverage played a crucial role in galvanizing public opposition to the war.

The Anti-War Movement and Public Dissent
As media coverage became more critical of the war, it coincided with the rise of the anti-war movement. Many Americans, especially younger generations, began to utilize the information provided by the media to organize protests and demand an end to U.S. involvement in Vietnam. College campuses became hotbeds of activism, with demonstrations often drawing thousands of participants. The media not only covered these protests but also helped amplify their messages, creating a feedback loop between public dissent and media coverage.

Television coverage of anti-war protests and the counterculture movement also influenced public sentiment. As reports of protests, marches, and civil disobedience proliferated, the image of the anti-war activist became intertwined with the broader narrative of the Vietnam War. This portrayal helped to humanize dissenters, showcasing them as passionate citizens rather than fringe radicals.

Conclusion
The role of the media in the Vietnam War was transformative, altering the landscape of warfare and public perception forever. Television and journalism provided a platform for both the realities of combat and the voices of dissent, creating a dynamic interplay that shaped American views on the conflict. The legacy of this media coverage continues to influence how wars are reported today, serving as a reminder of the profound impact that information can have on public opinion and policy. As we reflect on the Vietnam War, it is evident that media is not merely a passive observer but an active participant in the unfolding narrative of conflict.

The Anti-War Movement
The Vietnam War, a deeply contentious conflict, sparked one of the most significant anti-war movements in American history. This grassroots movement grew out of a complex interplay of social, political, and cultural dynamics, and it dramatically influenced U.S. policy and the eventual outcome of the war. The anti-war sentiment, which gained momentum in the 1960s, was driven by a combination of moral objections to the war, disillusionment with government narratives, and a burgeoning counterculture that rejected traditional norms.

At the heart of the anti-war movement was a profound moral opposition to the United States' involvement in Vietnam. Many Americans grappled with the implications of sending their sons into a war that appeared increasingly unwinnable and unjust. The televised images of gruesome battles, civilian casualties, and the devastation wrought upon Vietnam's landscape evoked widespread outrage and empathy. Activists argued that the war was not only a violation of human rights but also a misguided effort rooted in colonialism and imperialism. Prominent figures within the movement, such as Martin Luther King Jr. and Senator William Fulbright, publicly condemned the war, framing it as a moral failure that contradicted American values.

The anti-war movement was characterized by a diverse coalition of participants, including students, civil rights activists, intellectuals, and veterans. Organizations such as Students for a Democratic Society (SDS) and the Vietnam Veterans Against the War (VVAW) played pivotal roles in mobilizing opposition. The movement utilized various forms of protest, including marches, sit-ins, teach-ins, and public demonstrations. One of the most notable events was the 1969 Moratorium to End the War in Vietnam, which drew millions of participants nationwide and underscored the widespread discontent with the war effort.

Media coverage played a critical role in amplifying the anti-war message. As the conflict escalated, the media shifted from predominantly supporting the war to highlighting dissenting voices. Graphic coverage of the war's horrors, including the My Lai Massacre, galvanized public opinion against the U.S. government's actions. The stark contrast between official government reports and the realities depicted in the media fostered skepticism and distrust among the American public.

The anti-war movement's impact on U.S. policy was profound. As protests grew in size and intensity, political leaders faced increasing pressure to address public discontent. The Johnson administration initially attempted to downplay the movement, but as anti-war sentiment surged, it became politically untenable to continue the war without addressing public concerns. By 1968, with the Tet Offensive marking a turning point in public perception, the Johnson administration began to shift its strategy, eventually leading to a reduction in troop levels and a pivot toward negotiations.

The culmination of the anti-war movement's influence came with the 1970 Kent State shootings, where four students were killed during a protest against the war. This tragedy sparked outrage and further mobilized opposition to the conflict. As public pressure mounted, President Nixon announced the withdrawal of U.S. troops from Vietnam, effectively bringing an end to direct American involvement in 1973.

In conclusion, the anti-war movement played a crucial role in shaping U.S. policy during the Vietnam War. Through its moral arguments, grassroots activism, and strategic use of media, the movement not only influenced public perception but also pushed political leaders to reconsider their strategies. Ultimately, the widespread opposition to the war contributed to a significant shift in U.S. foreign policy and marked a pivotal moment in American history, highlighting the power of civic engagement and the importance of public dissent in democratic societies.

The Fall of Saigon and Its Consequences

The Fall of Saigon on April 30, 1975, marked a pivotal moment in both Vietnamese and global history, effectively bringing an end to the Vietnam War and leading to the reunification of Vietnam under communist control. This event was not merely a military defeat for the South Vietnamese government and its American allies; it represented the culmination of years of conflict, political turmoil, and societal upheaval that had profound and lasting implications for Vietnam and the world.

As North Vietnamese forces advanced towards Saigon, the capital of the Republic of Vietnam, the situation for the South Vietnamese government became increasingly desperate. The withdrawal of American troops in 1973 had left the South Vietnamese military to fend for itself, and despite receiving significant military aid, it struggled against the well-organized and determined North Vietnamese Army (NVA). The final offensive began in earnest in late March 1975, when the NVA launched a rapid series of assaults that overwhelmed South Vietnamese defenses.

The actual fall of Saigon was marked by chaotic scenes as civilians and South Vietnamese military personnel sought refuge in the U.S. embassy and other secure areas. Many were desperate to leave the country, fearing retribution from the advancing communist forces. The iconic images of helicopters evacuating people from rooftops encapsulated the sense of defeat and the end of an era for American involvement in Vietnam.

The immediate aftermath of the fall led to the formal reunification of Vietnam on July 2, 1976, under the banner of the Socialist Republic of Vietnam. This transition was not without its challenges. The new government faced the monumental task of rebuilding a war-torn nation. Estimates suggest that the Vietnam War resulted in the deaths of approximately 2 million Vietnamese civilians and around 1.1 million North Vietnamese and Viet Cong fighters, alongside 275,000 to 310,000 South Vietnamese military personnel. The devastation extended beyond human loss; infrastructure was in ruins, economies were shattered, and societal divisions ran deep.

In the years following reunification, the Vietnamese government implemented a series of socialist reforms, including land redistribution and the nationalization of industries. However, these policies initially led to economic difficulties, including food shortages and inflation. It wasn't until the introduction of the Đổi Mới reforms in 1986, which embraced market-oriented policies while maintaining a one-party state, that the Vietnamese economy began to recover and grow. This transformation eventually led to Vietnam becoming one of the fastest-growing economies in Southeast Asia.

The fall of Saigon also had ramifications beyond Vietnam's borders. In the United States, it marked a significant shift in public opinion regarding foreign interventions, particularly in military conflicts. The Vietnam War had already sparked widespread protests and anti-war sentiment, and the fall of Saigon solidified a sense of disillusionment. The perception that the U.S. had lost a war led to a period of introspection regarding American foreign policy, culminating in a more cautious approach to military engagements in the years that followed.

Internationally, the fall of Saigon signaled the triumph of communism in Vietnam, which inspired similar movements in other countries. The geopolitical landscape of Southeast Asia was altered, with neighboring nations perceiving the outcome of the war as a warning against U.S. intervention and a signal that communist movements could gain traction.

In summary, the Fall of Saigon was not just the end of a conflict; it was a transformative event with far-reaching consequences. It shaped the trajectory of Vietnam's development, altered U.S. foreign policy, and influenced global attitudes towards communism and interventionism. The legacy of this moment continues to resonate, reminding the world of the complexities and human costs of war.

Chapter 13

The Gulf War

The Lead-Up to War

The lead-up to the Gulf War, marked by Iraq's invasion of Kuwait on August 2, 1990, was a defining moment in modern Middle Eastern history. At the heart of this conflict lay a complex interplay of economic, political, and historical factors that escalated tensions between the two nations. Iraq, led by President Saddam Hussein, was burdened with significant debt following its protracted eight-year war with Iran, which had drained its economy and left it eager to restore its financial standing. Hussein viewed Kuwait, a small but wealthy neighbor, as a potential solution to his economic woes.

Kuwait's production of oil was particularly contentious. As a member of the Organization of the Petroleum Exporting Countries (OPEC), Kuwait had increased its oil output, which led to an oversupply in the market and a subsequent drop in oil prices. This situation aggravated Iraq's economic difficulties, as lower oil prices meant reduced revenues for an economy heavily reliant on oil exports. Hussein accused Kuwait of violating OPEC agreements by overproducing, which he claimed was a deliberate act of economic warfare against Iraq. He believed that controlling Kuwait would not only alleviate his country's financial strain but also enhance Iraq's position as a dominant power in the Gulf region.

The international response to Iraq's invasion was swift and multifaceted. Within hours of the invasion, the United Nations Security Council condemned Iraq's actions and called for an immediate withdrawal of Iraqi troops from Kuwait. Resolution 660, passed on August 2, 1990, marked a significant moment in international diplomacy, as it laid the groundwork for subsequent actions. The UN imposed a comprehensive economic embargo against Iraq, aiming to cripple its economy and pressure Hussein to withdraw his forces. This embargo reflected a broader consensus in the international community regarding the need to defend Kuwait's sovereignty.

As the situation escalated, the United States took a leading role in organizing an international coalition to confront Iraq. Under the leadership of President George H.W. Bush, the U.S. mobilized military forces in the region, signaling a strong commitment to uphold international law and protect Kuwait. The U.S. sought to build a broad coalition, drawing in support from countries across different regions, including Arab nations such as Saudi Arabia and Egypt, as well as Western allies like the United Kingdom and France. This coalition was significant not only for its military strength but also for its political legitimacy, as it represented a united front against aggression.

The diplomatic efforts culminated in UN Security Council Resolution 678, passed on November 29, 1990, which authorized the use of force to expel Iraqi troops from Kuwait if they did not withdraw by January 15, 1991. This ultimatum underscored the seriousness of the international community's resolve and set the stage for Operation Desert Shield, the precursor to Operation Desert Storm—the military campaign that would ultimately liberate Kuwait.

The invasion of Kuwait and the subsequent international response highlighted the complexities of Middle Eastern geopolitics, the significance of oil in global affairs, and the role of multinational coalitions in addressing regional conflicts. The Gulf War's lead-up demonstrated how economic pressures, national ambitions, and international diplomacy could converge, leading to a significant military engagement that would reshape the political landscape of the Middle East for years to come. The ramifications of these events would extend far beyond the immediate conflict, influencing U.S. foreign policy and regional dynamics long after the war concluded.

Operation Desert Storm

Operation Desert Storm, launched on January 17, 1991, marked a decisive phase in the Gulf War, aimed at liberating Kuwait from Iraqi occupation. The operation was the culmination of a meticulously planned coalition effort comprising 35 nations, led predominantly by the United States. The campaign was notable not only for its military strategy and execution but also for its display of international cooperation in response to aggression.

Strategic Overview

The military strategy behind Operation Desert Storm was based on the principles of overwhelming force and rapid maneuvering, known as the "AirLand Battle" doctrine. This approach emphasized the integration of air power with ground operations, allowing for a swift and decisive victory. The coalition forces, numbering around 540,000 troops, were equipped with advanced weaponry and technology, including precision-guided munitions, stealth aircraft, and extensive intelligence capabilities.

The initial phase of the operation was characterized by an extensive aerial campaign, known as Operation Desert Shield, which began in August 1990. This phase involved the buildup of coalition forces in the region and the strategic bombardment of key Iraqi military targets. The objective was to degrade Iraq's command and control capabilities, destroy its air defense systems, and cripple its military infrastructure. This phase lasted nearly five weeks, with a massive air assault that targeted critical installations such as communication hubs, military bases, and supply depots.

Execution of the Campaign

The execution of Operation Desert Storm itself commenced with a massive aerial bombardment that lasted from January 17 to February 24, 1991. The coalition launched over 88,000 sorties, delivering around 29,199 tons of bombs. The effectiveness of this air campaign was underscored by the use of precision-guided munitions, which allowed coalition forces to minimize civilian casualties and infrastructure damage while maximizing the destruction of military targets.

The coalition forces' air superiority played a crucial role in the success of the ground assault, which began on February 24, 1991. This ground phase, known as the "100-Hour War," involved a rapid advance into Kuwait and southern Iraq. Led by US General Norman Schwarzkopf, the ground forces executed a well-coordinated offensive, employing a strategy of flanking maneuvers to outsmart and overwhelm Iraqi defenses. The coalition forces used deception tactics, including a feigned attack to the south while launching the main thrust through the west, effectively outmaneuvering the Iraqi military.

Key Tactics and Outcomes

The tactics employed during Operation Desert Storm emphasized speed and flexibility. Coalition forces, including elite units such as the US Army's 101st Airborne Division and Special Forces, executed combined arms operations, integrating infantry, armor, and air support seamlessly. This approach allowed for rapid advances and the ability to exploit weaknesses in the Iraqi lines.

The operation concluded on February 28, 1991, with a decisive victory for coalition forces. Kuwait was liberated within just 100 hours of ground combat, and Iraq's military was devastated. The successful execution of Operation Desert Storm not only reinstated Kuwaiti sovereignty but also showcased the effectiveness of modern military strategies and technologies.

In summary, Operation Desert Storm represented a landmark moment in military history, illustrating the power of coalition warfare, technological superiority, and strategic planning. Its execution set new standards for future military engagements and redefined the international community's approach to collective security in the face of aggression. The operation's swift success underscored the capabilities of a united front against tyranny and served as a pivotal point in the geopolitics of the Middle East.

The Role of Technology in the Gulf War

The Gulf War, which took place from August 1990 to February 1991, marked a significant turning point in modern military history, largely due to the transformative role of advanced technology. As the United States led a coalition of forces against Iraq in response to its invasion of Kuwait, the integration of cutting-edge technology fundamentally altered the dynamics of warfare and set new standards for military engagement.

One of the most notable technological advancements during the Gulf War was the extensive use of precision-guided munitions (PGMs), commonly referred to as "smart bombs." Unlike traditional bombs, which had a high rate of collateral damage, PGMs offered the ability to strike specific targets with remarkable accuracy. This capability was crucial in minimizing civilian casualties and collateral damage while maximizing the effectiveness of military operations. The coalition forces dropped approximately 29,199 tons of bombs during the conflict, with around 8,600 of these being precision-guided munitions. The success of these weapons demonstrated their effectiveness in disabling key Iraqi military infrastructure, including command and control centers, air defense systems, and armored vehicles.

Another pivotal aspect of technology in the Gulf War was the use of advanced reconnaissance and surveillance systems. The United States employed a range of high-tech assets, including satellites, unmanned aerial vehicles (UAVs), and reconnaissance aircraft, which provided real-time intelligence and situational awareness. The ability to gather and analyze vast amounts of data allowed coalition commanders to make informed decisions on the battlefield, facilitating swift and coordinated strikes against Iraqi forces. For instance, the use of the U-2 spy plane and the Global Hawk UAV provided crucial information about enemy troop movements and positions, enabling coalition forces to exploit weaknesses in the Iraqi defenses.

The Gulf War also saw the introduction of advanced communication technologies that enhanced command and control capabilities. The coalition forces operated on a unified command structure that utilized secure satellite communications, enabling seamless coordination among the various branches of the military and allied nations. This technological integration was particularly evident in operations like "Operation Desert Storm," where air and ground forces worked in concert, leveraging technology to execute complex maneuvers and engage targets effectively.

Additionally, the employment of stealth technology played a crucial role in the Gulf War. The introduction of the F-117 Nighthawk stealth fighter, which could evade radar detection, allowed coalition forces to conduct night-time bombing raids with minimal risk of interception. The successful use of stealth aircraft underscored the importance of technological innovation in achieving tactical advantages on the battlefield.

Lastly, the Gulf War highlighted the impact of media technology, particularly the role of live broadcasting and satellite communications in shaping public perception of the conflict. The war was one of the first to be televised in real-time, allowing for unprecedented coverage of military operations. This media presence not only influenced public opinion but also served to keep the international community informed about the progress of the war, demonstrating the power of information as a strategic asset in modern warfare.

In conclusion, the Gulf War exemplified how advanced technology reshaped military strategy and execution. From precision-guided munitions and enhanced reconnaissance capabilities to improved communication systems and stealth technology, the conflict showcased the transformative effects of innovation on warfare. The lessons learned from this war continue to inform military practices and strategies in contemporary conflicts, underscoring the enduring importance of technological advancement in achieving military objectives.

The Aftermath of the War

The Gulf War, which commenced with Iraq's invasion of Kuwait in August 1990 and culminated in February 1991 with Operation Desert Storm, had profound and far-reaching consequences not only for Iraq but also for the broader Middle East and international relations. The immediate effects of the war were stark, as Iraq emerged from the conflict severely weakened, both economically and politically, while the geopolitical landscape of the region shifted dramatically.

Economic Devastation and Political Turmoil in Iraq

The war left Iraq in ruins, with extensive damage to its infrastructure and a staggering economic toll estimated at over $200 billion. The immediate aftermath saw the imposition of stringent economic sanctions by the United Nations, which were intended to prevent Iraq from rearming and to compel compliance with resolutions demanding the disarmament of weapons of mass destruction. These sanctions, however, had catastrophic effects on the civilian population, leading to widespread poverty, malnutrition, and a public health crisis. The suffering of ordinary Iraqis became a focal point of international discussions about the ethics and effectiveness of sanctions, raising questions about their humanitarian implications.

Politically, the aftermath of the Gulf War sowed the seeds for further instability within Iraq. The regime of Saddam Hussein, while initially emboldened by a sense of nationalism following the war, faced growing internal dissent. The brutal repression of uprisings in 1991, particularly in the Shiite south and Kurdish north, further entrenched the authoritarian grip of Hussein's Ba'ath

Party. This internal strife was exacerbated by the isolation imposed by the international community, creating a volatile situation that would fester for years.

Regional Implications and Power Dynamics

The Gulf War significantly altered the balance of power in the Middle East. The swift and decisive victory of a U.S.-led coalition effectively established American military dominance in the region, leading to a long-term U.S. military presence in Saudi Arabia and other Gulf states. This presence was viewed as a double-edged sword; while it provided a security umbrella for Gulf monarchies against potential threats from Iraq and Iran, it also fueled anti-American sentiment among various factions, including extremist groups.

Additionally, the war exacerbated existing tensions between Sunni and Shia populations in the region. The empowerment of Shia groups in Iraq following the war's conclusion and the subsequent sanctions against a Sunni-led regime contributed to deepening sectarian divides in the Middle East. This sectarianism would later manifest in various forms of conflict, notably during the Iraq War in 2003 and the Syrian Civil War.

The Impacts on International Relations

On the international stage, the Gulf War was a watershed moment that showcased the efficacy of multinational coalition forces and the United Nations' role in addressing aggression. However, the war also highlighted the complexities of international diplomacy. The subsequent perception of the U.S. as a dominant force willing to unilaterally intervene in the affairs of sovereign nations led to a backlash against American hegemony, particularly in the Arab world.

The aftermath of the Gulf War also set the stage for future conflicts, including the Iraq War in 2003. The unfulfilled promise of sanctions leading to regime change and the increasing focus on weapons of mass destruction as a justification for intervention would become central themes in U.S. foreign policy discussions.

In conclusion, the aftermath of the Gulf War had lasting repercussions for Iraq, reshaping its political landscape and societal fabric, while altering the dynamics of the Middle East and international relations. The lessons drawn from this period continue to influence contemporary discussions about military intervention, sanctions, and the quest for stability in a region marked by historical grievances and geopolitical rivalries.

The Gulf War's Place in Modern Military History

The Gulf War, which unfolded between August 1990 and February 1991, marked a significant turning point in modern military history, not only for its immediate geopolitical implications but also for its lasting influence on military strategy, technology, and international relations. The conflict, instigated by Iraq's invasion of Kuwait, prompted a swift and unprecedented coalition response led by the United States, demonstrating the effectiveness of multinational military collaborations in the post-Cold War era.

One of the most profound impacts of the Gulf War was the demonstration of the effectiveness of rapid deployment and high-tech warfare. The U.S.-led coalition, comprising 35 nations, showcased a remarkable ability to mobilize forces quickly, utilizing advanced technologies that had developed during the Cold War. The operation highlighted the potential of precision-guided munitions, which allowed for targeted strikes with minimal collateral damage. This shift towards "clean" warfare, where technology minimized civilian casualties and infrastructure damage, would set a precedent for future military engagements, leading to a paradigm shift in how wars were fought.

The Gulf War also underscored the importance of information warfare. The extensive use of media during the conflict transformed the way wars were perceived and reported. The 24-hour news cycle brought images of the battlefield into homes across the globe, shaping public opinion and influencing political discourse. The coalition forces effectively utilized psychological operations and media strategies to portray their actions as just and necessary, which would later inform military strategies in conflicts such as the Iraq War and the War on Terror. The role of media in shaping narratives around military actions became a critical consideration for strategists and policymakers, as they recognized the power of public perception in democratic societies.

Moreover, the Gulf War illustrated the complexities of coalition warfare. The diverse motivations of the coalition partners, ranging from economic interests to regional security concerns, highlighted the necessity for diplomacy alongside military action. While the coalition was united in its objective to expel Iraqi forces from Kuwait, underlying tensions among member states often complicated decision-making processes and operational coherence. This experience would inform the conduct of subsequent multinational operations, emphasizing the need for clear communication, shared objectives, and an understanding of the diverse political landscapes involved.

The lessons learned from the Gulf War also influenced military doctrine and strategy, particularly in regard to the use of air power. The success of the air campaign in achieving strategic objectives prior to ground operations led to a renewed focus on air superiority in subsequent conflicts. Military planners began to prioritize air power as a decisive factor in modern warfare, as evidenced in operations in the Balkans, Afghanistan, and Libya, where air campaigns were essential to achieving swift victories.

Additionally, the Gulf War's aftermath highlighted the challenges of post-conflict stability and reconstruction. The failure to establish a lasting peace in Iraq and the subsequent rise of insurgency foreshadowed the difficulties faced in later operations, particularly during the Iraq War (2003) and Afghanistan. This underscored the critical need for comprehensive post-war planning and nation-building efforts, an aspect that would become increasingly recognized in military doctrines worldwide.

In conclusion, the Gulf War significantly influenced modern military history by reshaping strategies, highlighting the importance of technology and media, and emphasizing the complexities of coalition warfare. Its legacy continues to inform military engagements in the 21st century, as nations navigate the evolving landscape of warfare marked by technological advancements, global interdependence, and the perennial challenges of achieving lasting peace.

Chapter 14

The War on Terror

The Origins of the War on Terror

The War on Terror, initiated in the aftermath of the September 11, 2001 attacks (commonly referred to as 9/11), marks a significant shift in the landscape of global conflict. The attacks were orchestrated by the Islamist extremist group al-Qaeda, led by Osama bin Laden, and involved the hijacking of four commercial airliners. Two of these planes were flown into the Twin Towers of the World Trade Center in New York City, resulting in the collapse of both towers and the deaths of nearly 3,000 people. A third plane struck the Pentagon, the headquarters of the United States Department of Defense, while the fourth, United Airlines Flight 93, crashed in Pennsylvania after passengers attempted to overpower the hijackers.

These unprecedented acts of terrorism shocked the world and represented a new kind of warfare—one characterized not by traditional military engagements between nation-states, but by asymmetrical conflict waged by non-state actors. The sheer scale of the devastation and the symbolic nature of the targets chosen by al-Qaeda highlighted vulnerabilities within the U.S. homeland and sparked an urgent call for action.

In response to the attacks, President George W. Bush declared a "War on Terror" on September 20, 2001, vowing to bring those responsible to justice and to prevent further acts of terrorism. This declaration was transformative, leading to a shift in U.S. foreign policy and military strategy. The immediate global response was marked by a surge of international solidarity with the United States, as countries around the world condemned the attacks and offered their support for military action against al-Qaeda and the Taliban, the regime harboring them in Afghanistan.

On October 7, 2001, the U.S., supported by a coalition of international partners, launched Operation Enduring Freedom, targeting Taliban forces and al-Qaeda training camps in Afghanistan. The military campaign aimed not only to dismantle these terrorist networks but also to establish a stable government in Afghanistan that would prevent the resurgence of extremist groups.

The war effort was justified under the premise of self-defense, invoking Article 51 of the United Nations Charter, which allows for the use of force in response to an armed attack. The United Nations Security Council passed Resolution 1373, which called on member states to work together to combat terrorism and enhance the legal frameworks against it. This marked a significant moment in international relations, as the global community began to recognize terrorism as a shared threat requiring collective action.

However, the War on Terror quickly expanded beyond Afghanistan. In 2003, the U.S. led a coalition to invade Iraq, citing the need to eliminate weapons of mass destruction (WMDs) and to address perceived threats from Saddam Hussein's regime. This decision was controversial and has been the subject of extensive debate regarding its legitimacy and consequences. The invasion of Iraq ultimately contributed to regional instability and the rise of insurgent groups, including al-Qaeda in Iraq, which later evolved into the Islamic State (ISIS).

The War on Terror has also led to significant changes in domestic policies, including increased surveillance, the establishment of the Department of Homeland Security, and the implementation of the USA PATRIOT Act. These measures sparked debates over civil liberties and the balance between national security and individual rights, raising important questions about the implications of such policies for democratic governance.

In conclusion, the origins of the War on Terror are deeply rooted in the events of 9/11, highlighting the complexities of modern warfare, the role of non-state actors, and the international community's response to terrorism. The repercussions of the War on Terror continue to shape global politics, security strategies, and societal attitudes toward conflict and peace in the contemporary world.

The Afghanistan Conflict

The Afghanistan conflict, particularly marked by the US-led invasion that commenced in October 2001, emerged as a pivotal moment in contemporary history, reshaping the geopolitical landscape of the region and altering international relations in profound ways. This military intervention was primarily a response to the devastating terrorist attacks on September 11, 2001, orchestrated by the al-Qaeda network, which was harbored by the Taliban regime in Afghanistan. The United States, under President George W. Bush, sought to dismantle al-Qaeda and eliminate the Taliban, which had provided them sanctuary and support.

The invasion was launched with a clear objective: to disrupt terrorist networks and free the Afghan people from the oppressive Taliban rule that had governed the country since the mid-1990s. The initial phase of the conflict was characterized by a rapid and overwhelming military response, with the US and its allies employing a combination of air strikes and Special Forces operations. These tactics aimed to support Afghan opposition groups, notably the Northern Alliance, which was instrumental in combating Taliban forces on the ground.

One of the most significant battles in the early phase of the invasion was the assault on the Taliban stronghold of Kandahar, which was both a military and symbolic victory for coalition forces. The swift capture of Kabul, the capital, marked the collapse of the Taliban government and the establishment of a new interim administration backed by the international community. However, the initial success of the invasion did not translate into a stable peace, as the Taliban quickly regrouped and began a protracted insurgency against Afghan and coalition forces.

The struggle against the Taliban evolved into a complex counterinsurgency campaign. The Taliban utilized guerrilla tactics, exploiting Afghanistan's rugged terrain and the socio-political fabric of the country, which included widespread distrust of foreign forces. The conflict increasingly drew in various regional and international stakeholders, complicating the situation. Neighboring countries, including Pakistan, played a controversial role, as their support for certain factions within Afghanistan influenced the dynamics of the conflict.

As the years progressed, the US and NATO forces faced mounting challenges. The Taliban's resilience highlighted the limitations of military power in achieving political stability. Efforts to build a viable Afghan government were hampered by corruption, ethnic divisions, and a lack of infrastructure, which led to disillusionment among the Afghan populace. Despite the significant investment in reconstruction and development, many Afghans continued to align with the Taliban, viewing them as a more reliable alternative to the perceived ineffectiveness of the Afghan government.

The conflict took a significant toll on the Afghan people, with civilian casualties rising sharply amid the fighting. The humanitarian crisis deepened, as millions were displaced, and basic services crumbled. The situation was further exacerbated by the resurgence of opium production, which became a critical funding source for the Taliban and other insurgent groups.

In 2011, the assassination of Osama bin Laden marked a symbolic moment in the conflict, leading to discussions about the future of US involvement in Afghanistan. However, the withdrawal of US and NATO forces, completed in August 2021, resulted in the rapid resurgence of the Taliban, which reclaimed control over Afghanistan just weeks after the last foreign troops departed. This abrupt change in power raised serious concerns about the future of human rights, particularly for women and minority groups, and the potential for Afghanistan to once again become a haven for terrorist organizations.

In conclusion, the Afghanistan conflict reflects the complexities of modern warfare, where military intervention often leads to unintended consequences. The struggle against the Taliban has illuminated the challenges of nation-building and the intricate interplay of local, regional, and global dynamics in conflict resolution. As Afghanistan continues to navigate its future, the lessons learned from this conflict remain critical for shaping international approaches to security and stability in war-torn regions.

The Iraq War

The Iraq War, initiated in March 2003, marked a significant turning point in modern military history and international relations. It stemmed from the broader context of the post-9/11 War on Terror, with the United States and allied forces targeting Iraq based on the belief that Saddam Hussein's regime possessed weapons of mass destruction (WMD) and had ties to terrorist organizations such as Al-Qaeda. Despite the lack of conclusive evidence supporting these claims, the U.S. launched a military invasion, leading to the swift toppling of Saddam Hussein's government.

The invasion began on March 20, 2003, with a campaign dubbed "Operation Iraqi Freedom." It was characterized by a massive aerial bombardment aimed at degrading Iraq's military capabilities and infrastructure. Ground troops, primarily composed of U.S. and British forces, rapidly advanced into Iraq, capturing key cities including Baghdad, the capital. Within just three weeks, on April 9, 2003, U.S. forces entered Baghdad, marking the fall of Saddam Hussein's regime. The images of jubilant Iraqis pulling down a statue of Saddam in Firdos Square became iconic, symbolizing the end of a brutal dictatorship that had ruled for over two decades.

However, the fall of Saddam did not bring about the anticipated stability or the establishment of a democratic government. Instead, the power vacuum created by the collapse of the Ba'athist regime led to widespread chaos and lawlessness. The de-Ba'athification policy, which aimed to remove Saddam loyalists from power, further exacerbated tensions. Many former officials and military personnel found themselves disenfranchised and resentful, laying the groundwork for a burgeoning insurgency.

As the initial euphoria faded, various insurgent groups began to emerge, fueled by sectarian divisions and a sense of national grievance against foreign occupation. Sunni and Shia communities, long suppressed and marginalized under Saddam's rule, began to vie for power. Disillusioned with the U.S. presence and the new Iraqi government, many Iraqis—particularly Sunnis—joined insurgent factions. These groups employed guerrilla tactics, including roadside bombings, ambushes, and attacks on coalition forces, leading to an increasingly violent and unstable environment.

The insurgency's complexity was further compounded by the involvement of foreign jihadists, including Al-Qaeda in Iraq, which sought to exploit the chaos. Their brutal tactics, including suicide bombings and sectarian violence, not only targeted coalition forces but also fellow Iraqis, intensifying the civil conflict. The situation reached a critical point in 2006 and 2007 when sectarian violence surged, resulting in thousands of deaths and displacements. The U.S. military responded with a "surge" strategy, deploying additional troops to stabilize the situation and support Iraqi security forces. This strategy yielded some success, reducing violence and allowing for greater political engagement among Iraqi factions.

Ultimately, the Iraq War resulted in profound consequences for Iraq and the broader region. The initial goals of establishing a stable democracy and eradicating terrorism were met with mixed outcomes. Iraq remained mired in violence and political instability, leading to the rise of extremist groups, most notably ISIS, which capitalized on the discontent and chaos that followed the war. The legacy of the Iraq War continues to influence U.S. foreign policy and strategies in the Middle East, raising critical questions about interventionism, nation-building, and the long-term consequences of military action in complex socio-political landscapes. The war's impact is a sobering reminder of the difficulties inherent in transforming societies through force, and it serves as a cautionary tale for future military engagements.

Counterterrorism Strategies

The war on terror, ignited by the devastating attacks on September 11, 2001, marked a significant shift in how nations address security threats posed by terrorism. In response to the evolving landscape of global terror, countries have adapted their military and intelligence strategies, employing a multifaceted approach that encompasses prevention, intelligence gathering, active engagement, and international collaboration.

1. Intelligence Gathering and Sharing

One of the foremost adaptations in counterterrorism has been the enhancement of intelligence capabilities. Nations recognized that effective counterterrorism relies heavily on accurate and timely intelligence. In the aftermath of 9/11, the United States established the Department of Homeland Security and the Office of the Director of National Intelligence to streamline intelligence operations and facilitate information sharing among various agencies. Internationally, organizations like INTERPOL and Europol have strengthened their roles, promoting cross-border intelligence sharing to detect and disrupt terrorist plots before they materialize.

Moreover, the rise of technology has revolutionized intelligence gathering. Surveillance techniques, data mining, and the use of social media analytics have become essential tools for identifying potential threats. Countries have invested in cyber intelligence capabilities, enabling them to monitor terrorist communications and online activities more effectively.

2. Military Engagement and Counterinsurgency

Military strategies have also evolved, shifting from conventional warfare to counterinsurgency and special operations. The U.S. military has employed a combination of ground forces, air power, and drone strikes to target terrorist leaders and infrastructure in regions like Afghanistan, Iraq, and Syria. The use of Special Forces units has become prominent, focusing on precision operations aimed at minimizing collateral damage while effectively dismantling terrorist networks.

Additionally, the concept of "winning hearts and minds" has gained traction, emphasizing the need for military forces to engage with local populations to prevent radicalization. This includes rebuilding efforts, providing humanitarian assistance, and supporting local governance to address the root causes of terrorism. By fostering stability and economic development, nations aim to diminish the appeal of extremist ideologies.

3. International Cooperation and Legislation

Counterterrorism has necessitated greater international cooperation. The global nature of terrorism means that threats often transcend national borders, requiring a unified response. Nations have entered into various treaties and agreements, such as the United Nations Security Council Resolution 1373, which obligates member states to prevent and suppress terrorist acts. Joint military operations, intelligence-sharing agreements, and collaborative training exercises have become common as countries work together to combat the threat.

Legislatively, many countries have enacted stringent laws aimed at curbing terrorism financing, enhancing border security, and enabling law enforcement agencies to act swiftly against suspected terrorists. These laws often include provisions for surveillance, data collection, and the prosecution of individuals involved in supporting terrorist activities.

4. Addressing Radicalization and Community Engagement

A comprehensive counterterrorism strategy also involves addressing radicalization at the community level. Nations have recognized that preventing terrorism is as crucial as responding to it. Programs aimed at deradicalization, education, and community engagement have been implemented to counter extremist narratives and provide support for at-risk individuals. Initiatives often involve collaboration with religious leaders, educators, and community organizations to promote tolerance and understanding.

5. Adapting to New Threats
Finally, as the nature of terrorism evolves—evidenced by the rise of lone-wolf attacks and cyberterrorism—countries continue to adapt their strategies. The emergence of digital platforms for recruitment and propaganda has prompted governments to develop counter-narratives and counter-operations in cyberspace to disrupt terrorist messaging and recruitment efforts.

In conclusion, the war on terror has driven nations to innovate and adapt their military and intelligence strategies extensively. This multifaceted approach, emphasizing intelligence gathering, military engagement, international cooperation, community involvement, and adaptability to new threats, reflects a comprehensive effort to combat the complex and evolving challenge posed by terrorism in the 21st century.

The Ongoing Global Impact of the War on Terror

The War on Terror, initiated in the aftermath of the September 11, 2001 terrorist attacks, has had profound and far-reaching effects on international relations, security policies, and civil liberties. This global campaign against terrorism has fundamentally altered the landscape of global politics and societal norms in ways that continue to resonate today.

Reshaping International Relations

The War on Terror has led to a significant realignment of international relations, particularly in how countries perceive and engage with one another. The United States, once considered a unilateral actor in global affairs, has increasingly sought multilateral partnerships to combat terrorism. This shift is evident in the formation of coalitions, such as NATO's invocation of Article 5 after 9/11, which marked the first time the alliance's collective defense clause was activated. Countries such as the United Kingdom, Australia, and Canada joined the U.S. in military operations in Afghanistan and Iraq, signaling a renewed commitment to collaborative security efforts.

However, the War on Terror has also strained relationships, particularly with nations in the Middle East and North Africa. The invasions of Afghanistan and Iraq generated significant anti-American sentiment and fueled regional instability. Countries like Iran and Syria, previously viewed through the lens of geopolitical rivalry, became pivotal players in a complex web of alliances and enmities shaped by the U.S.'s military presence and actions in the region. The resulting instability has contributed to the rise of extremist groups, further complicating international relations.

Evolving Security Policies

In response to the threats posed by terrorism, many nations have redefined their security policies, prioritizing counterterrorism measures over traditional military engagements. The U.S. implemented the USA PATRIOT Act, which expanded surveillance capabilities and law enforcement powers to monitor potential terrorist activities. This trend has been mirrored in various countries worldwide, leading to the adoption of similar legislation aimed at enhancing national security.

Furthermore, international cooperation on intelligence-sharing has increased, with nations recognizing the need to work together to combat transnational terrorism. Collaborative frameworks, such as the Financial Action Task Force, have emerged to combat money laundering and the funding of terrorism, illustrating a shift towards a more interconnected approach to security.

Impact on Civil Liberties

While the War on Terror has been framed as a necessary measure to ensure national and global security, it has also raised significant concerns regarding civil liberties. The expansion of surveillance programs, the detention of suspects without trial, and the use of enhanced interrogation techniques have sparked widespread debates about the balance between security and individual rights. In the U.S., the revelations by whistleblower Edward Snowden in 2013 about the National Security Agency's mass surveillance programs ignited a global conversation about privacy and government overreach.

The effects of these policies have not been confined to the U.S. Many countries have enacted similar measures, often justifying them in the name of national security. This has resulted in increased scrutiny of civil liberties, particularly for minority communities that may be unfairly targeted under counterterrorism laws. The implications of these policies raise pressing questions about the future of democracy and human rights in an era defined by fear of terrorism.

Conclusion

The War on Terror has reshaped the global landscape in profound ways, redefining not just international relations and security policies, but also the very fabric of civil liberties. As nations continue to grapple with the ongoing threat of terrorism, the challenge remains to balance the imperatives of security with the fundamental rights and freedoms that underpin democratic societies. The legacy of this conflict will undoubtedly influence future generations and the discourse surrounding conflict, peace, and the protection of individual rights in an increasingly complex world.

Chapter 15

Conclusion and Reflections

The Evolution of Warfare
Warfare has undergone significant transformations throughout human history, shaped by technological advancements, political ideologies, cultural shifts, and the evolving nature of societies themselves. This evolution reflects not only changes in weaponry and tactics but also the broader context of human civilization, including the rise and fall of empires, the emergence of nation-states, and the impact of globalization.

Ancient Warfare
In ancient times, warfare was predominantly characterized by hand-to-hand combat and the use of rudimentary weapons such as spears, swords, and bows. Armies were generally composed of infantry units, with cavalry playing a supporting role. The tactics employed were often straightforward, focusing on formations and the direct engagement of enemy forces. Iconic battles, such as those in the Peloponnesian War, relied heavily on the valor of individual soldiers and the strategic acumen of their commanders.

The introduction of organized military units and the concept of professional armies marked a significant evolution. The Roman legions exemplified this trend, as they combined rigorous training with innovative tactics, allowing Rome to dominate the Mediterranean. Furthermore, the advent of fortifications, such as walls and castles, began to change the dynamics of warfare, as sieges became a common strategy to conquer cities.

Medieval Warfare
The medieval period brought additional complexities, including the rise of chivalry and the feudal system. Warfare became more structured, with a clear hierarchy and the involvement of knights and noble families. The introduction of crossbows and later gunpowder weapons, such as cannons, transformed siege warfare and battlefield tactics. The Hundred Years' War between England and France showcased these changes, with longbowmen at the Battle of Crécy demonstrating the effectiveness of ranged weaponry against traditional knightly charges.

Additionally, the medieval period saw the emergence of naval warfare, with kingdoms vying for control of trade routes and territorial waters. The development of larger ships and improved navigation techniques allowed for more extensive maritime campaigns, setting the stage for global conflicts in the centuries to come.

The Early Modern Era

The early modern era witnessed the rise of centralized nation-states and the professionalization of armies. The use of gunpowder became widespread, leading to the decline of heavy cavalry and the rise of infantry formations armed with muskets and artillery. The Thirty Years' War exemplified the scale and destructiveness of this new form of warfare, as conflicts became increasingly intertwined with political and religious issues, demonstrating that wars were no longer just battles between armies but struggles for national identity and sovereignty.

The Industrial Revolution further revolutionized warfare through technological advancements. Railways enabled faster troop mobilization, while telegraphs allowed for improved communication on the battlefield. The introduction of machine guns, tanks, and aircraft during World War I marked a dramatic shift in combat, emphasizing speed, firepower, and mechanization.

Modern Warfare

In the contemporary era, warfare has evolved to include not only conventional armed conflicts but also asymmetric warfare, cyber warfare, and the use of drones. The Cold War introduced the idea of nuclear deterrence, fundamentally altering the nature of international relations and military strategy. Conflicts like the Vietnam War and the Gulf War illustrated the complexities of fighting in a globalized world, where media coverage and public opinion could significantly influence military strategy and outcomes.

Moreover, the War on Terror has brought about new challenges, as non-state actors like terrorist organizations employ guerrilla tactics and technology in unconventional ways. This shift has necessitated a reevaluation of traditional military strategies and the integration of intelligence, counterinsurgency, and humanitarian efforts into military operations.

Conclusion

The evolution of warfare reflects the dynamic interplay between technology, society, and politics. As we move forward, understanding this historical trajectory is crucial for grasping the current landscape of global conflict and for anticipating how future wars may be fought, shaped by emerging technologies and changing geopolitical realities. Whether through the lens of ancient battles or modern conflicts, the study of warfare remains a vital field that continues to inform our understanding of humanity's most profound struggles.

Lessons Learned from History's Biggest Wars

Throughout history, wars have served as both catastrophic events and profound learning opportunities, shaping nations and societies in ways that echo through time. The examination of major conflicts reveals critical lessons about human nature, governance, diplomacy, and the consequences of violence.

1. The Complexity of Causes:

One of the most significant takeaways from history's biggest wars is the multifaceted nature of their causes. Conflicts rarely stem from a single issue; they often arise from a complex web of political, economic, social, and cultural factors. For instance, the Peloponnesian War emerged from the rivalry between Athens and Sparta, underscored by issues of power, trade, and differing political ideologies. Similarly, the American Civil War's roots lay not just in slavery but also in economic disparities, states' rights, and deeply ingrained cultural differences. Recognizing this complexity is crucial for modern policymakers, emphasizing the need for comprehensive solutions that address underlying tensions rather than merely superficial symptoms.

2. The Role of Leadership:

Leadership has played a pivotal role in the outcomes of wars. Leaders can inspire nations to extraordinary feats or drive them to ruin with misguided ambitions. Figures like Winston Churchill during World War II exemplified the importance of decisive and resilient leadership in times of crisis. Conversely, poor leadership can exacerbate conflicts, as seen with various rulers whose decisions led to disastrous military campaigns. The lessons here highlight the necessity of effective leadership, not only in wartime but also in peacetime governance, to foster unity and resilience among populations.

3. The Human Cost of War:

Wars bring devastating human costs, both in terms of lives lost and the societal trauma that endures long after the guns fall silent. The staggering death toll of World War I and the Holocaust during World War II serve as stark reminders of the horrors of war. These events underline the moral imperative to seek peaceful resolutions and engage in conflict prevention strategies. The long-term psychological and cultural impacts on societies, such as the trauma experienced by Vietnam veterans and the ongoing struggles in post-war societies, further illustrate the need for comprehensive support systems for affected populations.

4. The Importance of Diplomacy:

History has repeatedly shown that diplomacy can be more effective than military action in resolving disputes. The Peace of Westphalia, which ended the Thirty Years' War, is a prime example of how negotiated settlements can lead to lasting peace. The lessons learned from failed diplomatic efforts, such as those leading up to World War II, emphasize the need for proactive and sustained diplomatic engagement to prevent conflicts before they escalate.

5. Technological Change and Warfare:
The evolution of warfare technology dramatically reshapes conflict dynamics. The introduction of machine guns and tanks in World War I and the use of nuclear weapons in World War II changed the scale and nature of warfare. Contemporary conflicts, such as the War on Terror, highlight the role of technology, including cyber warfare and drones, in modern military strategy. Policymakers must understand these technological advancements and their implications for future warfare, emphasizing the need for ethical considerations and international regulations.

6. The Fragility of Peace:
Finally, history teaches that peace is often fragile and requires ongoing effort to maintain. The Treaty of Versailles, which ended World War I, failed to establish a stable and lasting peace, ultimately leading to World War II. This underscores the importance of inclusive peace processes that consider the perspectives and grievances of all parties involved.

In conclusion, the lessons learned from history's biggest wars compel us to reflect on the nature of conflict and the human experience. By understanding the complexities of causes, the impact of leadership, the human cost, the importance of diplomacy, technological changes, and the fragility of peace, we can better navigate our contemporary global landscape and strive for a more peaceful future.

The Human Cost of War

War, in its myriad forms, has been a constant in human history, and its impacts resonate far beyond the battlefield. The human cost of war encompasses the direct toll on soldiers and combatants, the devastating effects on civilians, and the broader repercussions for societies and nations. Understanding this cost is critical for grasping the full significance of conflict in shaping human experiences and histories.

Toll on Soldiers
The immediate and most apparent cost of war is borne by soldiers. Combatants face not only the physical dangers of battle—where injuries and fatalities are common—but also psychological trauma. Conditions such as Post-Traumatic Stress Disorder (PTSD) have become increasingly recognized as a significant issue for veterans, affecting their mental health long after the fighting ends. The toll extends to their families, who must navigate the complexities of

reintegration into civilian life and the emotional scars that may accompany their loved ones. The sheer number of military casualties in major conflicts—World War I alone claimed over 16 million lives—underscores the brutal reality of combat and its lasting impact on those who serve.

Impact on Civilians

While soldiers are often the focus in discussions of war, civilians frequently endure the harshest consequences. Wars disrupt daily life, displacing populations, destroying homes, and severing community ties. Civilian casualties can sometimes surpass military losses, as seen in conflicts like World War II and the Vietnam War. The indiscriminate nature of modern warfare, with aerial bombings, artillery shelling, and urban combat, often results in tragic losses among non-combatants.

Moreover, wars can lead to humanitarian crises, including famine, disease, and lack of access to basic needs such as clean water and healthcare. The Syrian Civil War, for example, has resulted in millions of refugees and internally displaced persons, significantly straining neighboring countries and international resources. The psychological impact on civilians, particularly children, can be profound, leading to long-term issues such as anxiety, depression, and developmental challenges.

Societal Repercussions

The consequences of war ripple through societies, reshaping cultural, economic, and political landscapes. Economically, war can devastate infrastructure, disrupt trade, and drain national resources. Reconstruction efforts can take decades, as seen in post-World War II Europe or the aftermath of the Iraq War. The economic burden often leads to increased national debt, inflation, and reduced quality of life for citizens.

Socially, wars can exacerbate divisions within societies, leading to increased polarization and conflict. The aftermath of the American Civil War, for example, saw deep-seated racial and regional tensions that would take generations to heal. Wars can also result in shifts in power dynamics, leading to the emergence of new ideologies, movements, or regimes that may further impact citizens' lives.

Long-Term Legacy

The human cost of war extends into the future, influencing generations long after the cessation of hostilities. The collective memory of war can shape national identities, foster grievances, and influence foreign policy. Societies often grapple with the legacies of conflict, including the need for reconciliation, memorialization of losses, and the challenge of moving forward in the face of trauma.

In conclusion, the human cost of war is a multifaceted issue that touches every aspect of life. It is essential to recognize and reflect upon this cost, not only to honor those who have suffered but also to inform our understanding of peace and the importance of conflict prevention. As humanity navigates the complexities of modern warfare and its implications, fostering a commitment to peace and understanding remains an urgent necessity.

The Future of Warfare

As we enter an era defined by rapid technological advancements and shifting geopolitical landscapes, the nature of warfare is poised for profound transformation. The future of conflict will likely be influenced by several key factors: the rise of advanced technologies, the evolution of military strategy, the changing nature of alliances, and the complex interplay of national interests on a global stage.

Technological Innovations

Emerging technologies are set to redefine the battlefield. Artificial intelligence (AI) is at the forefront of this transformation, providing militaries with the capability to process vast amounts of data for strategic decision-making. AI-driven systems can enhance situational awareness, optimize logistics, and even automate combat operations, leading to faster and more efficient military responses. Unmanned aerial vehicles (UAVs) and drones are already being used for reconnaissance and targeted strikes, and their capabilities will only expand. The integration of AI in drone warfare raises significant ethical and operational questions, particularly regarding the accountability of automated systems in combat situations.

Cyber warfare represents another critical dimension of future conflicts. As nations increasingly rely on digital infrastructure, the potential for cyber-attacks to disrupt essential services, steal sensitive information, and manipulate perceptions has grown. The battlefield of the future may extend beyond traditional combat zones, incorporating cyber fronts where nations engage in espionage, sabotage, and psychological operations. The ramifications of such conflicts can destabilize economies and create widespread chaos without a single shot being fired.

Geopolitical Dynamics

Geopolitical tensions are likely to shape future warfare in significant ways. The rise of new powers, particularly China, and the resurgence of Russia as a military actor challenge the current world order. Competition for resources, territorial disputes, and ideological differences may lead to conflicts that are not only military but also economic and cyber in nature. As nations navigate this complex landscape, hybrid warfare—combining conventional military force with irregular tactics, cyber operations, and information warfare—will likely become a dominant strategy.

Moreover, the proliferation of advanced weaponry, including hypersonic missiles and autonomous weapons systems, raises the stakes of international conflicts. The potential for conflicts to escalate rapidly due to miscalculations or accidental engagements becomes increasingly plausible. The challenge of managing these risks will require enhanced diplomatic efforts and robust international agreements to regulate the development and use of such technologies.

The Role of Alliances and Global Governance

Future warfare will also be influenced by the evolution of military alliances and global governance structures. Traditional alliances, such as NATO, may adapt to address emerging threats and incorporate new technologies into their strategic frameworks. However, the increasing complexity of global politics means that alliances may shift, leading to new coalitions that reflect current geopolitical realities rather than historical ties.

Additionally, international organizations will face the challenge of addressing the ethical implications of modern warfare. As technologies like AI and autonomous weapons come into play, the need for a legal framework governing their use becomes paramount. The development of norms and regulations surrounding warfare will be crucial in preventing conflicts and ensuring that emerging technologies are employed responsibly.

Conclusion

The future of warfare is a complex tapestry woven from technological innovation and geopolitical dynamics. As nations grapple with these changes, the potential for conflict will be influenced by how effectively they can adapt their strategies, forge alliances, and establish governance structures that promote peace and stability. While the landscape may be fraught with challenges, the pursuit of diplomacy and international cooperation remains essential in mitigating the risks associated with the evolving nature of warfare. The lessons learned from past conflicts will serve as invaluable guides in navigating this uncertain yet pivotal future.

Final Thoughts on Peace and Conflict

Throughout history, wars have scarred humanity, leaving indelible marks on societies, cultures, and economies. As we delve into the narratives of the world's biggest wars, a recurring theme emerges: the profound need for peace and the urgent necessity to prevent future conflicts. The pursuit of peace is not merely an ideal; it is a fundamental requirement for the survival and flourishing of civilizations.

One of the significant reflections on the pursuit of peace is the understanding that the roots of conflict often lie in unresolved grievances, inequality, and the struggle for power. Wars frequently arise when nations or groups feel marginalized or threatened, leading to a cycle of retaliation and violence. Thus, fostering an environment of dialogue and mutual respect is critical. Diplomacy, negotiation, and conflict resolution mechanisms should be prioritized to address disputes before they escalate into violence. History has shown that proactive engagement can lead to the peaceful settlement of issues, as seen in various treaties that have successfully ended prolonged conflicts.

Moreover, education plays a pivotal role in the quest for peace. By promoting awareness of historical conflicts and their consequences, societies can cultivate a more informed citizenry that values peace over war. Educational initiatives that emphasize critical thinking, empathy, and cultural understanding can empower individuals to reject extremist ideologies and promote tolerance. In this interconnected world, the ability to appreciate diverse perspectives is paramount. The lessons learned from past wars illustrate the importance of understanding others' narratives to build a more harmonious global community.

In addition to education, the role of international institutions cannot be overstated. Organizations such as the United Nations were established not only to prevent wars but also to facilitate cooperation on global challenges like poverty, climate change, and human rights violations. A robust international framework that encourages collective action and holds states accountable can mitigate the conditions that lead to conflict. It is essential for nations to commit to multilateralism, recognizing that many modern threats transcend borders and can only be addressed through collaborative efforts.

The human cost of war is another critical reflection that underscores the importance of peace. The devastating impact on individuals—both soldiers and civilians—demands a concerted effort to prioritize human welfare over territorial or ideological ambitions. The psychological scars and the loss of life and livelihoods should serve as a constant reminder of the stakes involved in warfare. In this light, humanitarian efforts must be integrated into conflict resolution strategies to ensure that the voices of those affected by war are heard and considered.

Lastly, we must contemplate the future of warfare in the context of technological advancements. The rise of cyber warfare, drones, and artificial intelligence presents new challenges that could exacerbate conflicts or, conversely, provide avenues for preventing them. As nations navigate this evolving landscape, it is crucial to establish ethical standards and regulations governing the use of such technologies to avert unintended escalations and promote peace.

In conclusion, the pursuit of peace is an ongoing journey that requires dedication, empathy, and a commitment to learning from history's lessons. By fostering dialogue, investing in education, strengthening international cooperation, and prioritizing humanitarian concerns, we can work towards a future where conflict is minimized, and peace reigns. As we reflect on the past, let us embrace the hope that through collective action and understanding, humanity can indeed build a more peaceful world.